Living Spirit Forward

Learning to Live the Way You Were Meant to Live

By

Dr. Ron M. Horner

Gloria! Live this life! Ron

Living Spirit Forward

Learning to Live the Way
You Were Meant to Live

By

Dr. Ron M. Horner

www.CourtsOfHeaven.Net
PO Box 5847
Pinehurst, NC 28374
USA

Living Spirit Forward

Learning to Live the Way You Were Meant to Live

Copyright © 2021 Dr. Ron M. Horner

Requests for bulk sales discounts, editorial permissions, or other information should be addressed to:

LifeSpring Publishing
PO Box 5847
Pinehurst, NC 28374
USA

Additional copies available at www.courtsofheaven.net

ISBN 13 TP: 978-1-953684-12-7
ISBN 13 eBook: 978-1-953684-09-7

Cover Design by Darian Horner Design
(www.darianhorner.com)
Image: 123rf.com # 44054377

First Edition: February 2021

10 9 8 7 6 5 4 3 2 1

Printed in the United States of America

Table of Contents

Acknowledgements

The more we experience the realms of Heaven, the more amazed we are at the things Heaven unveils to us. The richness of the revelation is astounding. We are so grateful to those Heaven has made available to us the ability to gain insights that are impacting those who read and hear what we are sharing. To those who support LifeSpring International Ministries, thank you. To Donna Neeper, thank you. To my wife, Adina, and daughter, Darian, thank you.

Preface

Over the last several months, Donna Neeper (my Executive Assistant) and I have engaged Heaven on a regular basis as we have sought to understand more of the things of Heaven. A theme that evolved early in 2020 was to learn to "live spirit first." This book is a compilation of some of the things we have learned thus far about that concept.

In 1 Corinthians 14:26, the Apostle Paul writes that when believers come together, one would come with a teaching, another **a revelation**, another a song, and another a tongue or interpretation, so we need to understand that receiving revelation and then imparting it was a common practice in the early church.

Since everyone reading this book grew up in an age in which we are accustomed to the compilation of revelations which forms the Bible, the tendency is to think that new revelation ceased with the passing of the last writer whose material was eventually included in the canonized Bible. However, the personal experience of hearing the voice of the Father, Son, or Holy Spirit speak something to you, or reveal something to you through a dream or vision, still occurs. Revelation has not ceased; we have simply stopped being open to it.

As with all revelation, it will stretch you. Revelation revolutionizes. Revelation will unveil areas of your life where religious tradition has taken root. Many things we believe we have no scriptural basis for, yet we will defend those beliefs as if they came from the mouth of Jesus. Many times, we have not stopped to ask if a certain belief was truth or not. As you live as a believer, you should constantly be asking Holy Spirit to reveal beliefs that are not based in truth that you may have embraced.

If you read this book from your soul realm and read it as an intellectual endeavor, you will quickly put it down and denounce it. However, if you are hungry for a more intimate walk with the Father, then choose to tell your soul to sit back and call your spirit to come forward and invite Holy Spirit, who is our teacher and the one who will guide us into all truth. Let Him do the sorting and critiquing rather than your intellect. If you do these things, this book will benefit you. Your intellect is disqualified from judging spiritual things because it has been trained via the Tree of the Knowledge of Good and Evil, which places the intellect far above the spirit and was never designed to decide spiritual matters. It is outside of its created design.

We must understand that we are first and foremost a spirit being. We have a soul, and both soul and spirit reside in the earthly suits we call our bodies. The purpose

of your soul is to translate to your body what your spirit is perceiving and help you relate to the 3-D world we live in. We are instructed in Colossians 3:1-4 to live from our spirit, as opposed to living from our soulish realm. Allow Holy Spirit to witness to your spirit what is truth. Let us look at those verses:

> *See yourselves co-raised with Christ! Now ponder with persuasion the consequence of your co-inclusion in him.* **Relocate yourselves mentally!** *Engage your thoughts with throne room realities where you are co-seated with Christ in the executive authority of God's right hand.* [2] **Becoming affectionately acquainted with throne room thoughts will keep you from being distracted again by the earthly [soul-ruled] realm.** [3] *Your union with his death broke the association with that world; see yourselves located in a fortress where your life is hidden with Christ in God!* [4] *The unveiling of Christ, as defining our lives, immediately implies that, what is evident in him, is equally mirrored in you! The exact life on exhibit in Christ is now repeated in us. We are included in the same bliss and joined-oneness with him; just as his*

life reveals you, your life reveals him.[1] (MIRROR)
(Emphasis mine)

I know someone who often expresses the idea that if a concept were unknown to them, it therefore could not be true. How they came to this mindset I do not know, nor can I fathom, for many things exist in this earth realm that we do not know about. That does not mean they do not exist. The same is true for the soul realm, and even more so for the realm of the spirit. Just because I have never heard of something before does not mean that it is not true. It may have merely been outside my paradigm to date.

As you read through this book, understand that both Donna and I were stretched on many occasions by what we were learning and you will be stretched as well, but it will witness to your spirit as truth. We are eternally grateful to Heaven for the lessons we learned. I have found that the more I learn, the less I really know. Heaven has so much more to teach us.

What will Heaven be like?

Contrary to popular belief, we will not be going to Heaven just to be worshipping and playing harps all the time. Heaven is far more than that puny mindset. Will we worship? Yes. Will we be doing it continuously? I doubt it (at least in our present way of thinking) since Heaven is

---

[1] du Toit, Francois. Mirror Study Bible (p. 751) Kindle Edition.

another frame of existence. Heaven is so much more than we have been led to believe. Explore these revelations with us. They may answer some questions for you as well as lead you to a richer understanding of the love of our Father for us and the infinite provision available to us as His children.

In this book, we will share engagements with angels, men and women in white linen, Holy Spirit, and others. Engagements such as these are not uncommon, as they are visible throughout your Bible. However, religion has told us to "be careful," and religion is right. We must be careful *of religion* that keeps Heaven far, far away, and inaccessible until the end of one's life. We must also be careful of the doctrines of demons that tell us these things have passed away and we should not pursue them. Heaven is as close as your hand and has much to teach us about this earth realm. Let us be ready learners. We will discuss scriptural proofs concerning some of these things, so let your curiosity keep you engaged throughout the entire book.

It may be necessary for you to take a moment and search your heart for any belief system that causes immediate skepticism to arise within you. Religion has limitations. Some of them are built around the mindset that if organized religion did not teach it to you, then you should automatically reject it. On the other hand, it tells you that you must be careful, or you might get deceived. We can get deceived in our efforts to not be deceived. Some will cite the example of Joseph Smith and how he received a false revelation from the fallen angel Moroni.

Joseph Smith and his brother Hiram were active Freemasons and had already pledged themselves to be recipients of false light. Joseph Smith and his brother were predisposed to deception due to their covenants with Freemasonry. If you find that you have made covenants with darkness or you have a belief system that judges before any investigation, repent before the Lord, and ask the Father to open your heart to what He would have you learn. Heaven wants to reveal itself to you.

Understanding Veils

The understanding of veils is helpful to living spirit forward. Lydia, a woman in white gave this instruction, "The activity of going through the two torn parts of the veil (that tore at the crucifixion of Jesus) is the activity of the Kingdom where Jesus made the way accessible. It falls to the sons and daughters of God, just as it did to the priests who could only go there once a year, but now many can go, but we must engage and participate beyond the veil. You can imagine going between two pieces of torn fabric, but there are other ways to see the invitation that has been opened to you."

Donna had a dream once where she was walking through a warehouse full of carpets as if these carpets were hanging from the ceiling down to the floor and she had to move through them. "I was walking in a warehouse and I would come up to a thick, heavy rug, and I would have to push it out of the way, or I would have to pull it back or push it apart and step past it," she described. "In this warehouse I had to do this a couple of times and every successive veil that I went through (in the dream the carpets were veils) became progressively easier. I began to notice that the carpets were getting thinner and lighter. I could see through them and when I got through one after another, as I pressed through, Jesus met me, and He lifted the last veil for me, and I just came through it. I just cannot do it on my own."

We asked Lydia for clarification and she replied, "The discussion of veils let your readers know that the Kingdom of God is veiled. Jesus has made the way through, but the way of engagement is to step through the veil."

Donna was reminded of another dream where she saw a veil as if it were a very fine fabric. It was not a fabric like we would think—it was like the filament of a spider web, incredibly thin and woven together. She explained, "It went as high as I could see and went down to the ground, into the earth and it was like a screen made of this filament, and it was electrified because when, in the dream, I put my hand on screen, it vibrated and changed colors. It cycled through different colors of the rainbow in some pattern. As I looked at it, I could see when I put my hand out and felt the veil, or the screen, instead of looking at the screen, I could look through it and I could see things on the other side of it. That was a depiction of the Kingdom of God to me in that dream."

Lydia continued, "Help people understand that living spirit forward is living on the other side of the veil. You have this realm with the veil and then you have beyond the veil. Your invitation is to go through and beyond the veil. You can go through, your spirit can go through, but your body cannot, and your soul often cannot. Helping the readers entering into the realms of Heaven in this manner of description would be helpful."

The Value of the Soul

Within the pages of this book, I want it understood that I am not trying to convey that the soul is in any way unredeemable or unlovable. It is important to love your soul. By conveying spirit-forward living, we are not lessening the value of the soul. Jesus loves every soul. It is the use of spirit *first* that this book is primarily addressing and the increase of the spirit realm to live one's life connected to the Kingdom of God, and to know of which spirit you are. It is important to know your spirit is aligned and one with the Spirit of the Lord and that your spirit is a container of the Holy Spirit. This is important and helps with discernment.

The soul is the love of God and a place of rich treasure. It is highly valued in Heaven. It is one thing to talk about the soul as an object and another thing to talk about the operation of the soul while the soul is highly valued as a rich container that is able to accomplish many things in the physical. The operation of the soul before the spirit is a hindrance to the spirit of man who recalls its home in heavenly places.

As you read this book entitled *Living Spirit Forward,* may you be able to receive all that Heaven has to show you.

> *I pray that you would be blessed with an understanding heart and a willingness to explore Heaven on your own. May you be blessed with courage and boldness to pursue Heaven whatever the personal costs. May you be blessed with revelation on many levels. May clarity of things long misunderstood be granted to you. May you be willing to engage Heaven in fresh ways.*

Chapter 1

Recognizing Your Spirit

Your spirit (or spirit man) has existed since its creation by the Father, long before the earth was formed. At the moment of your conception, your spirit was inserted into your body (as tiny as it was) at that point in time and has been with you ever since. Your soul, the part of you containing your mind, will, emotions, and memories has not been activated quite as long. It became activated at birth, so your spirit has had an approximately nine-month head start on your soul.

However, because some of us did not even realize that we consisted of a spirit, that has a soul, that lives in a body, we never knew about activating it and how to live by our spirit instead of our soul. We have been poorly taught in those arenas, but hopefully this book will give you more understanding.

Modern psychology has certainly not helped either. It does not recognize the spirit as part of a person, so psychologists' efforts at understanding how we are made and how to help us get fixed when we are broken come up short because they are missing the most important part of the equation—our spirit.

Throughout this book, I will talk more about our spirit, how it functions and how it is designed, so I will not repeat myself here. Just understand that you have embarked on a journey that will change your life as you implement the principles taught in this book.

Many of us were taught that if we could not understand something intellectually, then that thing was not valid, which is a wrong concept. Regardless of whether your family, your school, your church, your friends, or even your society or government tells you that you must always reason things out and have those things fit in nice little boxes, our personal experience tells us differently. We have all had experiences that we could not explain, but that did not mean those experiences did not happen to us. I may not understand how electricity works, but it does not mean that I will not utilize it to turn on the lights in my home.

First Troubles

This problem started in the Garden of Eden when Eve was tempted to eat from the Tree of the Knowledge of Good and Evil instead of living out of relationship with God, the Creator. She and Adam had been living out of that relationship where they walked and talked with God in the cool of the day. Satan came along and enticed her with partial truths (which are not truths at all) and reasonings that God was holding something back from her. Well, that is true. He was trying to keep Adam and Eve from experiencing unnecessary trouble in their lives—troubles that were unleashed as soon as she took the first bite and swallowed it.

As a result of Adam and Eve's actions in the garden, the relationship and closeness with the Father was broken. Adam and Eve began living outside of their original design. They began to live from their soul. They came to know nakedness and shame, and not just physical nakedness or shame, but spiritual as well.

After their expulsion from the Garden of Eden, they came to know the sorrow of death as Cain killed his twin brother Abel. Cain came to experience banishment as a result of his uncontrolled jealousy. Mankind came to know fear, along with so many other things, as a result of Adam and Eve's sin. All these things were the result of living from one's soul and not from one's spirit.

Although we have been living out of our soul and out of our mental reasonings, we are still not happy or content. We were never designed to live just out of our soul realm. We are first and foremost spirit beings located on planet earth. Our soul was designed to help our bodies adjust and live in the physical world. Our spirit is designed to interface with Heaven and then instruct our soul in what it has gained from Heaven so that our entire being—spirit, soul, and body—are aided by what was learned by our spirit.

Ancestral Fears

We still battle fear thousands of years later. We are faced daily with situations in which we can succumb to fear, or we can overcome it. One of those fears occurs when we are faced with something new—it happens to us and it happened to our ancestors. In many cases, the fears of our ancestors have been passed down to us through our DNA and we find ourselves fearful of a situation when no rational reason exists for that fear. When we live out of our soul realm, we will often be faced with fear. Our adversary, the devil, will present us with opportunities to live and respond out of fear of something. The good news is that, as believers, we can live free of fear, but that necessitates us living out of our spirit and not out of our soul. If we recognize that we are living our lives out of fears inherited from our ancestors, we need to pause and repent for that.

Father, I recognize that I have been living out of the fears of my ancestors. I have been taught to fear the supernatural. I have been taught to fear things of the spirit and of the spiritual realms. Those fears have dominated my obedience to You and Your Word. I repent on behalf of the fears of my ancestors, I forgive them, bless them, and release them and I request to be released from the bondages these fears brought into my life as well. I repent for my own fear and ask your forgiveness. Open my heart to hear from You and from Heaven. I ask these things in Jesus' name.

Of course, some of us have our own set of fears that were developed in our lives without outside help. If Holy Spirit reveals these to you, just repent for coming into agreement with fear and request healing from the trauma of the event that brought it on and receive the peace that only Heaven can bring.

Each part of us is a realm. Our spirit is a realm, our soul is a realm, and our body is a realm. I will often refer to these as our inner realms. These realms are designed to interact with and complement one another.

The Apostle Paul instructed us to live from our spirit and indicated that if we did so, our walk would be ordered by Holy Spirit as well (Galatians 5:25). In Galatians 5:16, He let us know that if we choose to walk from our spirit (as opposed to our soul or flesh) we would not fulfill the desires of our soul or flesh.

*Living out of our spirit is far superior
to living out of our soul.*

When we choose to begin living out of our spirit which is the part of us most in touch with Heaven, we will be able to begin to experience Heaven in our own lives. We have been praying for this most of our lives as we have prayed the Lord's Prayer.

> *Your kingdom come. Your will be done on earth as it is in Heaven. (Matthew 6:10)*

When we pray this, we are inviting all the attributes of Heaven to be manifest (come into being) upon the earth. The goodness that is in Heaven we are inviting to come into the earth. The peace that is in Heaven we are inviting to come to the earth. The joy, the hope, the healing, the provision—all these things that are part of Heaven, we are inviting to come and be resident on the earth. The more focused we are on the things of the spirit realm, the more attuned we will be as these things manifest on earth and the more effective we will be in ushering them into the earth.

We also need to remember that often, our soul's emotions, intellect, and memories are behind veils. Sometimes these veils are due to fear or trauma. We must cleanse and removal these veils in order to engage Heaven and so our soul is free to hear from our spirit and work in tandem with our spirit. These veils, sometimes called "emotional interrupters," are lodged in the soul and cause a distortion of the soul.

The Spanish Speaking World

When we were writing this book, Heaven gave some insights concerning our wonderful Spanish-speaking audience. We tried to capture these thoughts so we could share with you how Heaven wants every bondage removed from the Spanish-speaking world.

Here is what Heaven shared:

"Often, Spanish speakers emote fiercely, but there is a current hook that prevents them from using their spirit first. Their spirit remains in a secondary position behind their soul. The emotion used against this population is a fear of moving in the supernatural due to the heightened awareness of the threat of evil beings. It is not that the Spanish populations do not believe in the supernatural— they do! But this fear is so in their blood and they believe in the negative part of the supernatural. They believe in the demonic side of it more than the angelic side of it. They will engage demons but draw back from engaging angels. They believe in the spirits on the land and of the land, and they are literally believing themselves to be under the powers of the principalities of the air who hold them captive and keep their spirit from moving with freedom.

If an evil being can get you
to fear them, they will have
the ability to dominate you.

"This is why the *Freedom from Mithraism*[2] book is so important. Overturning the false verdicts of Mithraism will greatly assist the Spanish population and will break

---

[2] *Freedom from Mithraism* by Dr. Ron M. Horner (LifeSpring Publishing) 2020.

off fear from them. That fear is often lodged in both their DNA and blood, causing them to think in terms of fear and subservience. It makes one think of oneself as a slave to the power of the air and one gives up hope that freedom could ever be achieved. They need to understand that this is in their generational bloodlines, which causes the soul to feel the emotion of that belief and causes fear—the fear of engaging the angelic and the light of Heaven due to long-held beliefs and the emotions that hold them captive.

"Because it is in the bloodline, they are essentially born with these fears passed down from their ancestors. However, they can be freed from these fears that have been passed down. Heaven can heal their DNA that has been damaged by these fears and traumas and they can live free of them.

"One of the beautiful things about Spanish speakers is that when they operate from the light of Heaven, they change their way of life dramatically. They really do—they no longer live under the dictates of fear, they make the needed adjustments, and they are free to enjoy operating in the supernatural with excellence once fear has gone or they have been freed from it."

Slave Ancestry

Another difficulty much of the Spanish speaking world—particularly in Central and South America—is the colonial ownership claims upon many of them, the native peoples' especially, though these claims can be on everyone in the population. Where their ancestors may have been considered the property of colonial powers in the past, for some people, these claims of ownership were never resolved in the Courts of Heaven.

Just as in America where those with slave ancestry still feel as if they are a slave, the reason is that in the arena of the spiritual world, legitimate ownership claims are still active. When President Abraham Lincoln issued the Emancipation Proclamation on January 1, 1863, it outlawed the practice of buying or selling of slaves or the owning of slaves from that point on. However, any slave purchased before that point in time (and not otherwise freed) was legally purchased according to the laws of the land. Therefore, the bill of sale was still lawfully in effect even with the Emancipation Proclamation. That aspect was never resolved in the most cases in the United States. In Great Britain, Parliament outlawed slavery and paid manumissions to the former owners, which released the bills of sale for the slaves they had purchased, but with few exceptions, that did not occur in the United States. The reason you may still be under the sense of slavery is that you were a legal heir of any covenants, agreements, or bills of sale that your ancestors were entangled with, and therefore, Satan holds you liable because the bills of sale are still outstanding. They must be resolved.

For those with slave ancestry, they often battle the same types of things. Slaves were not permitted to own property, they were not permitted to get an education, they were not permitted to own a business, a home, even a mule to farm with. None of their labor went to benefit them. When working with individuals with this ancestral history, I usually hear the same stories:

- They feel stuck in their job or career,
- They cannot own a home,
- They cannot have a successful business,
- They cannot get an education,
- They can never get ahead financially.

If you have slave ancestry, you will want to follow the same type of procedure listed below to obtain your freedom and get the bills of sale[3] absolved from off your life and your generations. Simply modify the following procedure to fit your situation.

Freedom from these claims is simple. Access the Court of Titles and Deeds and request that every ownership claim not arising from the Lord of Hosts be dissolved as it affects, you, your family, and your bloodline. Repent for any curses your ancestors may have placed upon those claiming ownership, forgive them for their sin, bless them, and release them of any spiritual debt. Sometimes, the ownership claim is from the Catholic Church, which has held power over the Spanish-speaking world for centuries. Other times, these ownership claims are from a government, especially if that government was communist or socialist in nature.

---

[3] You will likely have multiple bills of sales due to maternal AND paternal lines and sometimes multiple ownerships of the same slave ancestor.

These ownership claims manifest as garnishments on their increase. In the spirit realm, limits are placed on the individual's wealth. A ceiling is established upon their earnings power, so they are continually enslaved to the one(s) claiming ownership. Psalm 24:1 declares that the earth is the Lords and the fulness of it. He is the ultimate owner, not the Catholic Church or any other person or entity. In recent years, these ownership claims may have resulted from those assisting one in crossing national borders into another country. The fees charged to provide passage into the new country may have been exorbitant or may have required indentured servitude[4] as a form of repayment. Again, the Lord Himself is your ultimate owner—not a man or a group.

Some have experienced (or are under the influence of) dedications to the land or to the false deity Mother Earth, or something similar. Again, it is a false ownership claim that must be dissolved and marked satisfied by the blood of Jesus. As the Body of Christ repents and the population is redeemed from these claims, the people will gain freedom.

Aztec, Incan, or Mayan Ancestry

Another arena needing repentance concerns the oaths, sacrifices, and dedications made to Aztec, Incan, or Mayan gods. The evil trades made by ancestors have resulted in

---

[4] A contract between parties for supplying passage to another country. In exchange, the recipient would work to pay off the debt.

taxations upon the succeeding generations. Repentance for the ungodly trades, dedications of themselves or their children or animals, sacrifices of their children or animals (or any other type of sacrifices) need to be repented of. Then, in the Court of Cancellations, request the cancellation of every curse, oath, dedication, and false trading floor with which your ancestors or you have engaged in. Repent for their involvement and subservience to these false gods and receiving healing on every level from the damage done by these forms of profane worship.

Often sacrifices of children or animals were part of the rituals to these pagan gods. A person may make a trade with the pagan god in exchange for power, prominence, money, etc. The pagan god, usually working through a shaman, would demand the periodic sacrifice of a child as part of the trade. The person making the trade is expecting that they only need to make one sacrifice, however Satan usually has perpetual expectations. He expects payment (a form of taxation) every so many years throughout the generations. You will often see this when the firstborn child dies prematurely over several generations. That is a typical sign of a covenant of this type.

Repentance for Rebellious Strains

There is also repentance needed for rebellion that is related to their freedom that is ancestral in nature—even all the way back to the Tower of Babel that created a rebellious strain in their ancestry.

It is not that the Spanish-speaking peoples lack faith in the supernatural. It is that their faith is often focused on the wrong side of the supernatural and in the power of the deceived.

Forcing Religious Traditions

Another repentance would be to repent for forcing the younger generations to abide by religious traditions out of the fear that, if they do not, it will not go well with them. This has squashed the Spirit of God moving on the younger generations of Spanish-speaking nations due to the adamancy of parents and grandparents who put limitations on younger generations to flow with the Spirit of God out of the fear that, if this happened, they would receive retribution from evil powers. While this fear is based in some reality due to agreements of belief, the repentance is for forcing the younger generations to abide by religious traditions that mean nothing to them other than religious duty. The forcing of these religious traditions upon the next generations requires repentance, due to the bondages that came on the younger generation by the older generations who refuse to allow the change and movement of the Spirit of God within their nation, preferring to lean on their own understanding. They stayed true to religious bondages and thereby played a part in the capturing of their future generations by those same entities.

Many hunger to see their future generations freed from this and it is a deep-seated thing and they have not known how to get free. They cry out on behalf of the younger generation, but they have not known their role in setting that generation free.

Chapter 2

Learning to Live Spirit First

A challenge with how we were taught about the Christian life is that everything was put off until sometime in the future. Then, we read the letters of Paul and we experienced a disconnect. Heaven, to us, was a destination, not a resource. We knew nothing about learning to live from our spirits. We only knew what we had been doing all our lives, since birth, and that is to live to satisfy our soul or our flesh. We sorely need to learn an alternative way of living.

Exchanging Your Way of Living

Paul recorded these words in his letter to the Romans:

Those who are motivated by the flesh only pursue what benefits themselves. But those who live by the impulses of the Holy Spirit are motivated to pursue spiritual realities. (Romans 8:5)

We must learn to live spirit first! We must exchange our way of living. We must learn to live from our spirit. We need to understand the hierarchy within us:

- We are a spirit.
- We possess a soul.
- We live in body.

Each component has a specific purpose in our lives. Our spirit is the interface with the supernatural realm. It is designed for interfacing with Heaven & the Kingdom realm. Your spirit has been in existence in your body since your conception. Your soul has a different purpose. It communicates to your intellect and your physical body what your spirit has obtained from Heaven. It is the interface with your body. Your body houses the two components and will follow the dictates of whichever component is dominating,

Most of us have never been taught about having our spirit dominate. Rather, we have merely assumed that our soul being dominant was the required mode of operation.

Our soul always wants to be in charge. Our soul is susceptible to carnal or fleshly desires, lusts, and behaviors. It will, at times, resist our spirit and body. It must be made to submit to your spirit by an act of your will.

Your will is a means of instructing either component (spirit, soul, or body) what to do. Your soul has a will and so does your spirit. You choose who dominates!

Your body, on the other hand, has appetites that will control you in subjection to your soul. They become partners in crime—remember that second piece of chocolate cake it wanted? Your body will try, along with your soul, to dictate your behavior. It will likely resist the spirit's domination of your life. However, it will obey your spirit's domination if instructed, and your body can aid your spirit if trained to do so.

The typical expression that operates in most people's lives is that their soul is first, body second, and their spirit is somewhere in the distance in last place.

In some people, especially those very conscious of their physical fitness or physical appearance, there is a different lineup. Their body is their priority, the soul second, and again their spirit is the lowest priority.

Heaven's desire for us is vastly different. Heaven desires that we live spirit first, soul second, and body third. Since we are spiritual beings, this is the optimal arrangement. For most of us, our spirit was not activated in our life in any measure until we became born again.

If, after our salvation experience, we began to pursue our relationship with the Father, then we became much more aware of our spirit and learning to live more spirit conscious. The apostle Paul wrote in his various epistles about living in the spirit or walking in the spirit. Because we are spiritual beings, our spirits cry out for a deepening of relationship with the Father. Our spirit longs for it and will try to steer us in that direction.

Our soul has certain characteristics that explain its behavior in our life. This is the briefest of lists, but I think you will get the idea. Our soul is selfish. It wants what it wants when it wants it. It can be very pouty. It can act like a small child. It is offendable and often even looks for opportunities to be offended. Our soul is also rude.

Our body has a different set of characteristics. It is inconsiderate, demanding, lazy, and self-serving. It does not want to get out of bed in the morning, for many people. In others, it wants to be fed things that are not beneficial.

However, characteristics of our spirit are hugely different. If we live out of our spirit, we will find that we are loving and prone to be gentle. We desire peace. We are considerate. We are far more contented when living out of our spirit. Also, joy will often have great expression in our lives.

Sometimes we have experienced traumas that create a situation of our soul not trusting our spirit. The soul blames the spirit for not protecting it. The irony is that typically, our soul never gave place to the spirit so that it could protect us. The soul places false blame on the spirit and it must be coerced to forgive the spirit. Then the soul must relinquish control to the spirit. Once the soul forgives the spirit, the two components can begin to work in harmony.

If I were to flash an image of some delicious, freshly cooked donuts in front of you, what would happen? For many, their body would announce a craving for one. What if, instead, I showed you an image of a bowl of broccoli?

How many people would get excited about that? Probably not as much excitement over a bowl of broccoli would be exhibited. Which does your body prefer—the donuts or the broccoli? For the untamed soul, the donuts are likely to win out every time. Which do most kids prefer?

In any case, you can train yourself to go for the healthier option. A principle regarding this that I heard years ago is summed up like this:

What you feed will live—
what you starve will die

What do we want to be dominant—our spirit, our soul, or our body? The part we feed is the part that will dominate.

For some, they feed their soul and live by the logic of their mind. Everything must be reasoned out in their mind before they will accept it. However, because our soul gains its insight from the Tree of the Knowledge of Good and Evil, it will always have faulty and limited understandings.

How do we change this soul-dominant or body-dominant pattern? We instruct our soul to back up and we call our spirit to come forward. Some people may need to physically stand up and speak to your soul and say, "Soul, back up," and as they say those words, take a physical step backward. Then, speak to their spirit out loud and say, "Spirit, come forward." As you speak those words, take a physical step forward. This prophetic act helps trigger a shift within them.

Live spirit first!

Benefits of Living Spirit First

Why would you want to live spirit first? Let me present several reasons to you. Living spirit first will create in you an increased awareness of Heaven and the realms of Heaven. It will create a deeper comprehension of the presence of Holy Spirit, and of angels and men and women in white linen. You will be able to better hear the voice of Heaven. You will experience greater creativity, productivity, hope, and peace. You will become more aware of the needs of people that you can meet.

As you live spirit first, you will be able to access the riches of Heaven in your life. Petty things that formerly bothered you will dissipate in importance or impact in your life. You will be able to move ahead, not concerning yourself with the petty, mundane, or unproductive things that have affected your life before you began to live spirit first.

This way of life is more than a game changer—for the believer, it is the only way to live. You will face challenges as you build your business or live your life from Heaven down, but you will more readily be able to access the solutions of Heaven as you live with an awareness of the richness of Heaven and all that is available to you as a son or daughter of the Lord Most High. I encourage you, do not live dominated by your soul. *Live spirit first!*

Chapter 3

Understanding

Living By Your Spirit

The focus of our ministry has been teaching people how to understand and work successfully in the Courts of Heaven for the last several years. However, in the last year we had noticed a broadening of what we do as a ministry. Heaven explained what we were experiencing as we engaged with Heaven recently.

Heaven shared, "Living by one's spirit will not be optional for Sons of God in the earth in coming days. You have had several months to learn some of the principles of living by one's spirit. I am broadening your perspective to be not just the Courts of Heaven but also the realms of Heaven and how to live out of those realms. The two are intertwined and must be learned about by the saints.

"The saints are the ones to adjudicate as the ecclesia. You are not *victims* of 'negative' political climates, but you are beacons of light amid darkness. The saints in the United States were not as effective in governing as they should have been the last four years. They were like preschoolers coming into a new school yard that did not know how to utilize the things on the playground, nor did they know how to use the tools in the library or in the classrooms.

"The declaration Donna shared is critical for living spirit forward." This was merely a daily instruction she gives to her soul and her spirit. This is essentially what she does each morning:

> *I speak to my soul this morning and instruct you to surrender your position in ruling my inner realms to the spirit. Soul, I appreciate what you do, but today we are going to yield to my spirit who will be working in conjunction with Holy Spirit.*
>
> *Body, you will cooperate with my soul and especially my spirit. Today, we are going to have a good day.*

Heaven explained, "You are giving the instruction to your soul AND spirit of how the day is going to be. It is not a struggle for your spirit to receive that, yet it is typically a struggle for your soul. Your soul must see the benefits of living soul back and spirit forward. Unless you allow the rest that comes from Heaven to come forward, you will not experience the fullness of your spirit and soul working in tandem or as a unit. The soul is not your enemy; it is simply poorly trained in spiritual things.

"The way people have their soul behave religiously happens when they succumb to religious spirits or demons that focus on those things from a standpoint of false piety. That is a poor substitute for how the sons are supposed to live.

---

*Live from your spirit **TO** your soul.*

"Let your spirit impart to your soul, not the other way around. The soul's information, as well-intentioned as it might be, is contaminated by many things that are not fruitful. Your spirit was designed for the ongoing presence of God, whereas your soul is simply the interface for your body to interpret and receive the signals delivered to it by the soul or communicate to your spirit the needs of the body. If your soul has no input from your spirit, then the input it receives is from outside sources and therefore not usually helpful.

"Many try and fill the spirit with good things, but your spirit will get a sort of indigestion from things not designed for it. Communion with the Father is what it longs for. It is the yearning of the spirit, not the soul—although many songs have phrased it that way because the writers did not understand the role of the soul versus the role of the spirit.

"When Paul says to not live after the dictates[5] of the flesh, he is not just speaking of the physical body, but of the physical body dictated to by the soul in the person that has a dormant or inactive spirit. Many people go their

---

[5] Galatians 5:16-17

entire lives with their spirit essentially dormant. This dormancy creates a boredom within a person that is hard to shake off. Only when their spirit is called to attention and awakened do they begin to come alive. Aliveness is what it is designed for.

"In Ephesians 5:14 where it says, 'Awake you sleeper get up!'—that is speaking of the dormant spirit that has been allowed to sleep. The spirit is where the light of Jesus is to shine from, not the soul. That is what that passage speaks to. Similar verses say the same type of thing. Isaiah 60:1 says, 'Arise, shine—be light'. It is speaking to the spirit, not the soul. The soul will awaken to whatever feeds it—good or bad. Therefore, you must be careful of what you feed it.

Remember, what you feed will live and what you starve will die.

"Be mindful of what you are feeding on and what you are feeding it with. The wrong diet will produce the wrong results. Feeding the wrong part of you will result in wrong results as well. Live *by* your spirit and *for* your spirit, not from your soul. Your spirit will not neglect the soul to its detriment when the spirit is being fed properly. It will see that the soul is taken care of and receives what it needs.

"Some things only the spirit of a man knows how to deal with and cannot be easily translated to the soul, but the spirit will find a way to administer it to the soul, so the soul receives the benefits of the impact of the information given by the spirit."

Paul's Understanding

Paul understood living by one's spirit and taught extensively on it. However, the challenge for believers in this day is to come to right understandings of your sonship with the Father. The training of the vast majority of the Body of Christ is that you were born in sin, so your duty is to sin, and you are in a constant battle with your fleshly carnal nature to not sin, rather than merely living in righteousness before the Father.

To live righteously is to simply live out of who you are not who you have been told you are from the religious establishment.

As the sons and daughters understand *who* they are and *whose* they are, their mindsets will shift to a more positive one than what they have embraced. Every "-ology" they have lived by will change—for the better.

To live from one's spirit will be the result of a decision to do so.

You speak to your soul to take its rightful place in the hierarchy and obey the instructions coming from your spirit. Your spirit has been made alive through the resurrection power of Jesus. It understands living this way. It is your soul that has trouble moving ahead. The

Word says, "You has He quickened,"[6] or breathed life into—resurrection life—so that you can move forward in a new way of living and being. As you live from resurrection life, you will be changed on an ongoing basis.

Many things have been put in place by world systems, religious systems, and the wiles of men, but they are not ever the final word. The Father is the owner of this world and He has the final word. He never surrendered His rulership to another. He allows certain things to play out, but surrender is not on the table. To surrender is to suggest one is victorious and the other a loser in conflict. It is to suggest one is dominant and greater in power than another. No contest exists between the two. God has no equal as far as opponents.

A remnant of sons and daughters has always existed that is not getting smaller but is getting larger, stronger, and more filled with the wisdom of God and the understandings of Heaven. Living out of one's spirit is crucial for maximizing the resurrection life. To live that way is simply an embrace of what has been done for you by the Father and the Son.

False Belief Systems

Layer by layer, the false belief systems that have infiltrated the church will be dismantled in the lives of His yearning ones. These yearning ones are those who hunger

---

[6] Colossians 2:13

and thirst after the presence of the Lord of Hosts. They hunger after His righteousness that they are told to seek after in Matthew 6:33. You not only have righteousness, but you are also told to seek it. Righteousness is the right understanding of your sonship. If you understand your position as a son, your thinking will be right, your actions will be right, the words of your mouth will be right, the attitudes of your heart will be right. You will see yourself as the Father sees you, one of inestimable worth and incalculable value because you are His peculiar treasure. You are His desire in the earth. To see you recognize who you really are will bring Him the greatest of delights. That is what He yearns for in His sons and daughters, so He places a reciprocal yearning in His sons and daughters to know Him and be known by Him. It is this reciprocal desire that works to draw you closer and closer. As you draw closer, the gravity pull of His desire pulls you even closer to Him. You have an example of this with the gravitational pull of the earth and the moon. The pull is stronger the closer they get to one another and as you orbit who He is, your view of Him changes, your perspective changes, and your desires change, for you want to do nothing that would displease Him and put you at a distance from Him. As you move toward Him, you see Him more clearly, more acutely, than you would at a distance. Pictures of this process are all about you. His desire for you is all around you. He wants you to know Him more than you want to know Him for yourself, but as you stay in the warmth of the glow of His presence, the unnecessary things are shed from you. They fall off you never to be picked up again because His desire is FOR you.

The understanding that Jesus died *AS* **you** is crucial to understanding the impact of the work on the cross that was accomplished. Justice would cry out and say that humanity on its own merits was not qualified or able to offer the necessary bloodshed for the remission of their sins. Their guilt would have been too strong upon their lives, as they know the things they had chosen to do which were outside their true identity.

To succumb to sin is to succumb to a form of action outside of your identity. You were fashioned from the Father's hand to be a certain way. Because of the corruption of sin upon humanity, things occur that bring humanity off-balance with who they really are. You have seen it in the lives of others you have known where their environment was a tremendous drag upon their discovery of who they are were meant to be. Those who never deal with the things of their generations and the things in their own past can never get past those attachments. Only if they were to submit themselves wholly on a long-term basis and willfully choose to pursue the heart of the Father day by day, moment by moment, could they possibly free themselves from the many things of their past that hinder them daily. They can submit to the continual cleansing work provided by their attachment to the vine.

Fragmentation

Environments that humanity exposes themselves to often cause an increase in the depth of the depravity they find themselves in. The constant exposure to outside negative forces coupled with the impacts of trauma upon their lives where doors are opened and invaders take up residence is another part of the environmental aspect of their lives, or where trauma results in fragmentations.

The fragmentation and disjointedness of a soul that many have experienced (and for some, a fragmentation of their spirit) has been little understood in the Body of Christ, as they did not see how such fragmentation could have been possible. However, evidence of fragmentation is all around us. It is in nature with the brokenness in forests. It is in their homes with brokenness, disarray, and uncertainty concerning what they should do. For some, their lives are out of order, while for others, they have their lives overly structured, which is the remainder of their soul crying out for normalcy and completeness.

A certain degree of soul normalcy is needed for people to experience. When that is out of place, they are not able to function at a normal capacity. As I noted in my book, *Engaging the Courts of Healing & the Healing Gardens,* trauma's primary purpose is to induce fear into the person's soul. Once the fear is introduced, many other things can be allowed and wreak havoc—not, only in them, but also in their homes, families, careers, and more.

Last year, we ministered to a young woman who had been severely broken. Part of the brokenness was real, while other parts were agreed to by her soul. Just as you can create casualty covenants with physical conditions, you can read about someone's brokenness through SRA or other traumatic events and then put yourself in agreement with the symptoms or characteristics and find yourself susceptible to the brokenness the enemy would seek for you. You can begin to exhibit similar symptoms to those who have experienced ritualized abuse and similar events. This has happened to more people than we realize. Theirs is assumed brokenness because it seemed similar to their experience when they read of another's experience, heard it in a message or through a testimony, and took hold of it. These casualty covenants work on the physical plane, so it stands to reason they can occur on a different plane. So it is with fragmentations of soul and spirit.

Refreshing for the Soul

When your soul is tired, it is often because your body is tired or because you have had many things working on your emotions around you. Your soul must be refreshed. When you have instructed your spirit to go to the Gardens of Heaven for refreshing, and you have instructed it to gain refreshing and then deliver it to your soul, you also need to have it delivered *from* your soul *to* the body. Your body can only get so much rest from sleep and non-activity. It does not receive all it needs without the input of the soul from the spirit. They are interconnected. We have not understood this interconnection of spirit, soul, and body, but Heaven will grant us some understanding so we will know how to live properly with all parts engaged. Once these principles are in place, we will be much more refreshed, and our body will be rejuvenated in a much better fashion than is currently happening.

You have seen and read the scriptures where it declares that your body is the temple of the Lord[7] and Holy Spirit lives within that temple within your spirit. He does not live within your soul or your physical body. However, three-dimensional thinking cannot typically grasp it any other way. Your body is the reservoir for both soul and spirit, but as a reservoir, it must have an inlet and an outlet to function properly.

You feed your body with food and nutrients—that covers the outside sources of nutrition, but the spirit can also feed the body. Remember when Jesus said the things that defile a man come from within—the things proceeding from the heart? Evil imaginations and unholy appetites are from within and do much more damage than unwashed hands. Things coming from within can also cleanse and heal the body. These things must come through the spirit.

The bridges between your inner realms—between spirit and soul and between soul and body—must be maintained and kept healthy. The soul, because it is accustomed to being the dominant inner realm, will often step over into gatekeeping mode when it is simply a communication pathway from one inner realm to the next in the sequence Heaven designed. When it acts as gatekeeper, it has stepped outside its boundary and will

---

[7] 1 Corinthians 3:16

create situations for disease and lack of health. It is to be a conduit, not a controller. It is a gate and not a gatekeeper. It is the pipe, not the faucet.

For instance, when you are in a situation where an anointing for physical healing is in place, Holy Spirit moves upon your spirit, who, in turn, moves upon your soul with the message, "I have that healing the human has been desiring." Yet, because of the woundedness of the soul in some arena, it refuses to allow the healing gift to flow into the body from the soul. Instead, it tries to hijack it for its own benefit. Yet, because it was not a healing flow for the emotional arena but for the physical, the healing is never able to manifest in your body. Selfishness of the soul created the closure of the gate, stopping the flow of healing intended for your body. It made itself to be God in your life and shortchanged the working of Heaven in response to the cry of your heart. Selfishness is a common foe of which the soul is often guilty. The body can be guilty as well, as is evidenced by the cravings for certain dietary things.

It is a matter of the soul being unwilling to give up its dominating position. The soul was never designed to be in charge of your inner realms. It is ill-equipped to do so, because it lacks the realm of the spirit and the wisdom and insight coming from that realm. Without the input of the spirit in one's life, one faces an emptiness and a lack of satisfaction with all they do. They can experience a measure of pleasure and joy, but because the equation of the spirit is left out of the mix, the person can never truly experience a "fullness" of joy. The greatest portion is always missing.

The soul must be taught to surrender its position. You can instruct it as a matter of your will, but if you explain the benefits of its surrender, it will accomplish more. Think of it like you were having to reposition someone in a company you owned because their skillset was inadequate for the task—you can remove them forcibly, or you can explain the need for the growth and benefit of the company and explain that they are not being fired, but are being repositioned to a place more in keeping with their design. They will still have input, but they will no longer be in dominance over You, Inc. They may pout a bit, but, given no option, they will succumb to your instruction as CEO of You, Inc. Honor what they have done in your behalf, but also recognize that it is not time to be overly compassionate. It is time to make the necessary changes so you can accomplish all that is in your scroll. Let the soul understand that it has a part to play and that you honor that part, just as you honor the body for its part that it plays in your life. However, it is time for the real boss— the real Director of Operations—to take His place in your life.

> *Your scroll cannot be accomplished when your soul is dominating. It can only occur when the spirit is dominating in your life.*

Your spirit has access to the information center of the Seven Spirits of God. It has already been programmed with that information source. Yet, because you have been taught that you are not to live by your spirit, you have not done so and have been without the resources of the Seven Spirits of God. Their input will only be accessible when a hunger for their input is desired or you have an openness to it. This may come by the words of your mouth, or simply by the cry of your heart for wisdom, understanding, counsel, might, knowledge, or the fear of the Lord, with the Spirit of the Lord Himself in His fulness ready to manifest in your life and situation. It is this heart cry that brings the Seven Spirits of God to attention.

Heaven explained, "David understood the value of the heart cry. He would cry out often in His pursuit of the Father's heart. The heart cry also meant that he found Me when he cried out to me." He apparently succeeded in his cries to the Father, for Acts 13:22 records him as one who had the heart of the Father. "So, it is with everyone who will cry out to me. I will be found by you."

Seek the Lord while He may be found, call upon Him while He is near. (Isaiah 55:6)

Our Five Senses

As your spirit receives from Heaven, it is responsible to enlighten your soul realm as to what it has gained from Heaven. For that reason, it is imperative that we learn how to hear from Heaven with our 5 senses. We were created with a sense of sight, hearing, touch, taste, and smell. We have the same senses within the inner realm of our spirit. Our body contains the mechanism for our natural senses to operate, but our soul is what attaches the emotions and memories of the experiences of smell, hearing, taste, touch, or sight, so we can appreciate their aroma (regarding pleasant things) and learn to avoid the unpleasant ones.

We may enjoy the fragrance of a rose, but not be nearly as excited to smell the odor of a skunk, a small animal whose primary defense mechanism is the ability to release a very unpleasant smell. Both can be pungent, but one will be far more pleasant than the other.

We can hear from Heaven. We can see things from Heaven using our spirit eyes, we can smell, taste, and touch heavenly things. We can attune ourselves to these things by training. Often with hearing, we will hear the still small voice of Holy Spirit speaking to us just as Elijah did on mountain.[8] We can see things in visions just as Ezekiel did.[9] We can taste the flavors of Heaven as David mentioned in Psalm 34:8. As the woman with the issue of blood who touched the hem of Jesus' garment, she touched more than the cloth He was wearing, she touched Heaven and received her healing.[10] Her body cried out for relief, her soul was in agreement, and her spirit facilitated the encounter.

---

[8] 1 Kings 19:12
[9] Ezekiel 1:1
[10] Matthew 9:20

Later in this book, we will give four simple keys to hearing from Heaven so that you can learn to record what Heaven is speaking to you. Heaven wants to speak to you. Heaven wants to show you many wonderful things and as we engage from our spirit and not from our soul, we can begin to experience Heaven in a whole new way.

Chapter 4

Cooperation of Your Realms

Garzan[11] said, "I will speak plainly to you. Your adversary already has counterfeit shifts in place that are already defeated, but your enemy does not believe they are defeated. Therefore, he will continue in his own deception to try to shift the Bride to wrong geographical locations or direct the Bride in a wrong manner. Therefore, we (the angels) will need to do battle, which we are capable of doing and skillful at. Our directive from the King is to keep the Bride receiving the truth of His revelation so that His Spirit and His might will be demonstrated in days ahead."

He continued, "The people of God must refrain from fear regarding revelation and *must commission their own angels to do battle at their realm gates* so that the enemy is overwhelmed. Then he smirked and said, "Angels are so much more powerful than angels of darkness and

---

[11] Garzan is an angel who assists Ezekiel, the ministry angel.

demons! You need to rely on these angelic beings to help you receive the truth of the revelation through portals that are going to be opened in this hour."

Eradicate Fear

Then Garzan said, "Remind the people **they are to have nothing to do with fear**. They must eradicate fear from all their realms and look for where their realms may be holding on to fear. Realms that hold fear are like the corruption on a data file. It must be purged and cleansed. That is what will be happening to the Bride as she works her way through this shift of becoming more led by the Spirit of God within her human spirit." He said, "I speak to you on two levels—both corporately and individually."

Back to Basics

He continued, "I am going to go back and talk basics: It is possible for the body realm to have held fear in the DNA, as well as it is possible for the soul realm to have fear born of emotion. It is also possible for the spirit realm to have fear or to contain fear, simply by having agreed with fear. It is easy for a Spirit-filled believer to cast fear out of one's spirit by looking at the truth of the beauty of the kingship of Jesus. This is the daily feeding of the spirit man with the character of God as revealed through His Word.

The soul realm is more difficult to eradicate fear from because fear hides within one's emotions. Often though, it hides in manipulation and in control. All these are born of a spirit of fear, which is not native to you or to your soul realm. The body realm is a similar thing.

Bridges to the Spheres

He then began showing two bridges.

Garzan began, "If you look at your realms as spheres lined up in a line, you have a bridge between your spirit and your soul, then a bridge between your soul and your body. From these realms, things cross back and forth on these bridges. Notice that, in order for the body realm to receive something from the spirit, it must go through the soul. Similarly, the spirit can receive something from the body realm, but it also must go through the soul. This is why the soul must be cleansed, understand who it is, and understand its role. It is not the leader. In your internal realm are internal bridges—the soul being the communicator between the three. It is a communicator between the realms."

Next, he showed an image of one's realm as if they are spheres within spheres. He continued, "The innermost sphere is the spirit, the next sphere is the soul, and then you have the sphere of the body. This is how the container of the body works in the physical realm of earth created by God. We are given a body vessel to contain a soul vessel to contain a spirit vessel.

"Therefore, being spirit-led from the inner man, in which the inner human spirit is connected to the Kingdom of God—which is the inner most sanctuary of God who dwells within you richly—can be communicated outward through the soul, to the body. Often, when the human spirit is receiving from the Holy Spirit in the realm of the Kingdom, it does not reach the body level because the soul contains it and does not let it go out to the body realm, but it can."

Ezekiel said, "These are mysteries, but mysteries have solutions. Do you remember when Jesus was on earth? He spoke in parables. A parable tests the soul to engage it with a mystery, to give opportunity and invitation to pursue the meaning from the spirit realm, not from the natural realm. Metaphors in dreams do this as well. The son or daughter of God, who is led by the Spirit from their awakened human spirit, comes into a more perfect alignment leading from the spirit to the soul, and then to the body.

Many people can get stuck thinking the physical realm is the primary realm, when it is the spirit (otherwise known as the inward man) that is the primary realm. The spirit has the might of God, the counsel of God, the wisdom of God—all seven spirits mirrored within the spirit of man. The one who has an awakened spirit receives from the seven Spirits of God. The Seven Spirits of God reflect outward through the soul, then to the body, and from the body to the physical realm.

You carry the Kingdom
of God within you at all times
[in the inner man, the human spirit].

Your soul communicates this to your body and as your body comes into agreement and alignment with the inner man (the spirit), the release of the Kingdom in the physical realm can then occur. Healing and other things can manifest.

"This looks like a demonstration of the power and might of God. This is what Moses did when he raised his staff and the earth responded. Not only that, as he raised his staff at the Red Sea, the angels of God, hearkened to the staff Moses was given as his authority symbol and took up their positions in the unseen to hold back the waters."

Ezekiel continued, "I tell you a great mystery. This is coming to earth again. These will be called the signs and wonders of God and will operate through those who are operating from their inner man. The Bride is learning,

43

and, as you have known, some are forerunners. They are the demonstrators of what is possible.

"You have seen how little children become frustrated when they know they should be able to tie the laces on their shoes, but after several attempts, their laces remain untied or loose to the extent where they are quickly untied. Frustration sets in and for a time that child does not even *try* to tie the shoelaces. Then a moment of a reasoning happens when their being steps through and the contradiction of why other laces can be tied, but he is not able to tie his laces occurs. The contradiction of this catapults the effort to try again, and after practice, the laces become tight. The result is joy and the feeling of accomplishment." Ezekiel said, "I tell you; this is a similar pathway of the Bride, as she learns to release the Kingdom of God on earth."

At that point we paused to commission Ezekiel and his ranks as we had been instructed:

Ezekiel, we commission you, your commanders, and your ranks, to guard the portals of revelation that are being opened by the book that was just released, so that what is received is received by the spirit, not by the soul of those individuals who read it.

We commissioned you to direct the courses to the spirit of the revelation, so the spirit guides the heart to the soul.

We commissioned you to guard the portals of the book and the season for those portals to be open. We commission you to patrol, to perform sentry duty, to do battle at the gates, to overcome the twisting of illegal lies that want to shift the revelation and cause confusion about the revelation that has been released. We commission you to be alert and use all the authority given to you by Heaven to perform these duties and to bring revelation and wholeness to pass in those who read the book in Jesus' name."

Living Water

As we continued, Ezekiel had a silver pitcher in his hands. It was very large and had a handle and a spout. "This is a container of living water," he explained. "This is the courses that are poured out from Heaven through revelation portals. Some individuals have small pitchers, while others have large pitchers. Tell the people to be content with the living water being poured out within their spirit vessel, so that they may pour it out in their geographies to those they influence.

"Do not judge others too harshly or too quickly," he explained, "or judge the measure of their flow." (He was not talking about judging the content and was talking about the comparison trap.) He continued, "Do not judge the flow quantity of the living water through another person's pitcher, but ask the Lord to increase the flow, for

He is good. As you prove to be a worthy vessel, you will gain more."

He finished by saying, "You have a saying that you do not give a young child the car keys to a vehicle. This is true in Heaven as well."

Chapter 5

Living Spirit Forward

Donna explained, "What I heard Heaven say to me this morning when I stepped into Heaven was the word 'winds.' I saw a kite and then a person who was flying the kite who started talking to me about winds. He said, 'There are many winds. They are like currents and they are being released from Heaven and you can get in one.'"

The analogy was that a wind current is just like a river current. It will take you somewhere. Get in the spirit and determine if there is a wind you want to get into and you can do so, whether it is a wind of revelation or a wind of comfort. These winds are winds you can step into in the realms of Heaven. You could step into the Kingdom of God in your spirit and experience what wind (or winds) are blowing there. Donna continued explaining that she felt like the Father releases angels' winds to the physical realm. It is like a current here (discernible by one's spirit) and she could probably get in it. She thought, "It would be good for me if I would receive the wind currents that are being brought." It brought to mind the verse in Hebrews: "He makes his spirits winds, his ministers a flame of fire," (Hebrews 1:7).

We then began an engagement with Mitchell, a man in white who came and began by asking Donna, "What was the last thing that Heaven told you this morning?"

She replied, "Heaven told me that a current is flowing from Heaven through my spirit man that I could get in, like on the back of kite, and I could flow with that wind."

Mitchell said, "That is correct. This is a spirit-forward activity."

He continued, "From your spirit man, you choose the wind (or winds) you want to receive from. These winds are ministering angels that are released to the dimension of the earth.

These winds must be received
from the spirit in the spirit.

"They come near to assist with the lifting up or the raising up of one's spirit to a current that is not the present current of earth or not the present current of the soul realm.

Earth operates on the soul realm
through the interaction of humanity.

"But spirits awakened by God have the opportunity to ascend to different currents that are being released from Heaven and remain in those currents. This is a spiritual activity.

"A spiritual activity is one of *focus* where you become aware of where your spirit man could potentially focus. Direct your spirit to that place. The soul needs to understand what the spirit knows. It needs to get training from the spirit. The spirit of man gets training and receives comfort, peace, and joy, and is watered and fed by the Holy Spirit from the Kingdom realm. However, the enemy of your soul hopes you never find this avenue, even if you are born again, so that your spirit man is not filled by Holy Spirit or awakened to gain strength to flip your manner of life to spirit-forward living from soul-led living.

The soul often is adjudicating things from the physical realm based on intellect and emotion and memory–these memories are often linked to mindsets of youthful experiences.

"The soul realm can be functioning well in the 3-D world, but *the component of the spirit is imperative for spirit life.* An awakened spirit hears from God. An awakened spirit hungers for the things of God. An awakened spirit can be both hungry, thirsty, in need of fellowship, in need of love, and in need of companionship. These are the things your spirit man has need of. Many people get these confused with their soul and often their soul is confused with their spirit.

"Your spirit is a realm filled by the power of God, filled by companionship with Jesus, companionship with the Father, companionship with Holy Spirit. Your spirit is the receiver of the Seven Spirits of God and their functionality and what they are releasing. Your spirit is the light that causes other spirits to be touched and awakened. Thus, *ministry from the spirit is much better than ministry from the soul.*"

Mitchell continued, "In order for the power of God to be released into the earth the spirit of the man must be engaged to receive that power and might of the Holy Spirit and direct it. It has to be directed. It can be directed in intercession, in conversation, through the body, or by the laying on of hands, but all these things are sourced from the spirit of the person. The soul and the spirit have been redeemed unto the Father.

The Father's pleasure is that your spirit
is in communion with Him,
His Son, Holy Spirit, Heaven, and those
dwelling now in the Kingdom of God.

"You call these the great cloud of witnesses such as I. I am one of those. Your discipline of relationship is to be childlike, hungry, thirsty, and willing.

"The enemy will often use the will of the soul to interrupt what the spirit is willing to do. This takes discipline, practice, and feeding on the Word of God to know one's identity in order to overcome the resistance the enemy is using within the soul realm," Mitchell stated.

Soul Realm Distractions

"Many beliefs exist in mankind at this time. It has not always been this way, but it is right now. There are many soul realm distractions," he continued. "One such distraction is soul realm edification—the thing that your soul goes to or turns to in order to get edified (like everything from excitement to food)." He explained, "I'm giving examples of some good things that your soul will allow itself to receive from. These are not necessarily bad, but rather out of balance, and if the soul is not aligned properly with the spirit and the way the spirit experiences this, you are not living in your full identity or at your full capacity.

"The life of Jesus has much to be studied to look between the lines and allow Holy Spirit to teach you how Jesus lived as a man with an awakened spirit in conjunction with Holy Spirit and with the flow of might and power of the authority of the Kingdom of God. Notice that this was even before He went to the cross for the payment of all sin. Similarly, the disciples and the 70 who were released by Jesus to minister were first taught who they were and then released with instructions." He said, "The instructions you read in the scripture are a few of them. What they did was they walked in the spirit, trusting the power and might of the flow of Holy Spirit (within

51

their spirit), along with winds and currents to heal the sick and carry out many authorities against the enemy." (Luke 10:1-24)

Mitchell added, "Do you remember when Ron was describing the image of the three realms of a person in a line with bridges connecting them, and how a healing anointing may get stuck in the soul? Holy Spirit explained that what is in the soul that gets in the way He calls 'mind genuflections.'[12] Your mind in your soul is bowing down to a preconceived notion or something you thought. Instead of surrendering to that, do not bow down, do not pay homage to that thing you were taught, but allow the healing to flow through the conduit of the soul to your body realm so that the body realm receives what the might and power of God is releasing."

"I find the phrase 'mind genuflection' to be such an interesting phrase," Donna interjected, "because you get that picture of a person bowing down to an idol, or to a religious tradition, or to something they thought that they just have not rethought, or they had not surrendered to the potential for a rethinking on it. We are walking in such an age of that right now with portions of the body of Christ being assisted in new thoughts about that."

Mitchell explained, "I am not too concerned that you struggle so hard to get some of this understanding. I am confident that this is all coming out in the perfect timing of God. Just the sowing of seed to people regarding their

---

[12] Genuflection: bowing of the knee

spirit being and getting them thinking about the different operations of their being is breaking off religiosity and religious thinking and helping them to begin to really consider how personal one's spirit can be with the personality of the Son, the Father, and Holy Spirit.

"When you move from the place of living from your spirit, nothing is impossible. It is the atmosphere of Heaven. When you move in that realm and you teach your soul to sit down and rest because you are going to operate from the place that has no impossibility, you are going to sooner or later connect that to how it manifests in the earth.

"Dwell on these things in the realm of the current of winds where nothing is impossible," Mitchell encouraged us. "Dwell in a current of joy, a current of abundance, a current of blessing, a current of building, a current of creativity. These are winds released from Heaven. Receive these winds into your spirit realm and tell your soul to be affected by this spirit realm and by what the spirit realm knows as it is affected in the currents in which it is flowing."

Ezekiel (the angel of the Ministry), who had just appeared, interjected, "Get into winds of being comfortable, speaking to angels, learning from angels, partnering with angels, and engaging angels in the spirit for the things they do well. I am going to tell you that your soul can be concerned with something Heaven is not concerned about, and when you feed that part of your soul and you feed on those concerns that Heaven is not concerned with, your attention and your focus is very easily and quickly shifted to look and live from the natural realm.

"Living from the natural realm is problem-oriented. It is solution-oriented. Living from the spirit realm is not solution-oriented. It is possibility-oriented. It is 'nothing is impossible-oriented.' It is not finding a solution; it is *receiving* the solution. Believers have walked in grace for a long time where, without knowing their spirit was helping them, they were receiving creative ideas and understanding. It is not like this is brand new, but the potential and the opportunity and the greatness of it is."

Operating from Your Spirit

Donna abruptly laughed when hearing what Ezekiel said next and she remarked, "I get called out by Heaven all the time."

Then Ezekiel said to Donna, "Haven't you just been thinking that operating in things that you do all day long from the spirit realm ought to be easier? Your thinking is that it would be so much simpler to do all of this from the spirit and not get stuck in the soul where the soul begins to feel weary. You can say to your soul:

'You may feel weary because you're trying to do something that you are not meant to do, so we are going to step over to the spirit realm. We are going to let our spirit lead, and we are going to fly through these activities. We are going to be

54

assisted. We are going to have angels speak to us and the Kingdom of God participate with us.'

"This happens from the spirit man," he said. "Don't worry. It is just a matter of learning to practice that, of learning that it is available and then learning to do it and to stay in it. That is what the winds help with and help you stay in it and stay on it."

Letting Your Soul Operate

Ezekiel continued, "You will have times for your soul to be in operation. For example, if a feast in the physical realm is being prepared, then you need your soul to engage the fellowship of the feast, the taste of the food, the flow of the conversation, the enjoyment of the moment.

"Now, imagine that in the same scenario where you are engaged with your spirit. Your spirit does not necessarily take the first position but assists the soul in processing what is going on. Some call this looking beyond, looking between the lines, looking with spirit sight, or looking in the spirit to see what also is taking place. Then from this position, you see angels, you feel them, you taste the river of God, you see the goodness of His participation with you at the feast. When you do things this way, is not your enjoyment much more magnified because you have engaged the soul *AND* the spirit realm, because Father made you this way? Therefore, if you ever feel in a stuck place, engage to see which realm you are operating out of and switch to the other, and then agree that they can

55

communicate one with the other. You can do both, you can live from both."

Engaging Angelic Assistance

Since Ezekiel had been assisting us in this engagement, it seems fitting to bring in another aspect you will want to include in learning to live spirit forward. Commission your angel(s) to assist you in living spirit forward. It can be a simple as this charge to your angel:

First, call them near. Once you sense their nearness, commission them:

> *I commission you to assist me today to help me live spirit forward. You are commissioned to remind me and keep me in peace should my soul want to arise. I welcome your assistance this day, in Jesus' name.*

The Flesh is the Flesh

Ezekiel explained, "The flesh is the flesh. (He is talking about the body side of our beings). The flesh is always going to follow what the soul and spirit are doing, believing what the soul believes, unless it is in second place behind what the spirit is feeding upon. There is a manifestation of the flesh that is behind the other two realms. Therefore, if a belief system in your spirit is communicated to your soul and your soul is in agreement and surrenders to the belief of the spirit, the body benefits

56

by receiving from the soul what it has agreed with in the spirit, and it will manifest—but it will take *time* to manifest in the physical realm. It does not happen instantly. Very often it happens in what you would call a gradual manner, but it does happen, and you can look for it. Many are impatient, expecting the physical realm to operate in the same parameters that the timelessness of the spirit operates in. Be patient. Be kind to your flesh.

"I will give you an example," Ezekiel went on. "Your soul has recognized, from your spirit, a need to change your diet. I am talking about the natural food you put in your body. The soul first has to go through a phase where it is willing to surrender the things that it has believed, such as wrong information about nutrition, or emotional conditioning to things that are not healthy. As the soul aligns with new patterns of thought, you can get the spirit involved. The spirit will help the soul stay in the realm of a changed mindset and eventually, you will find yourself feeding your body differently and, from that, the body will ultimately benefit. This is a pretty common thing to talk about, but you may not have seen it from the three realms of you."

Our Spirit and Worship

Mitchell began pointing out another nuance. He said, "The spirit has the capacity to see itself like the Father. This next thing I will share is linked to worship. It is linked to why we worship. Our spirit worships in that it focuses upon where it came from, what it truly is, who is responsible for that, which would be the Creator—Yahweh. It would be the Almighty God. It would be the living resurrected one. The spirit worships because it receives benefit and empowerment by focusing spiritual senses on the character of God from which one's spirit came. Is this not truly seeing who you are?

Worship helps you see who you are
by seeing who He is.

"People who struggle with identity issues often struggle with worship because they are using the wrong eyes to determine their identity. They are using natural eyes to try to determine who they are instead of their spiritual eyes to see who He is, and to see yourself mirrored in a reflection of who He is; seeing which facet of Him you are most like comes from the spirit activity of praise, worship, relationship, companionship, and affection for the spirit realm, for the Godhead, for the unseen."

Fear in Hearing

Then Mitchell said, "Do you want to know why people don't journal when you ask them to journal what they hear? They are afraid they are going to hear something negative. They do not hear something negative, but they are afraid that they are going to hear something negative, and they believe this in their soul, and it shuts down their spirit from hearing. This is the needed work of cleansing the soul.

"If the soul does not communicate the power and might of God to the body, it is because the soul has fragments. It has broken places and woundedness. It not only has fear, it contains fear as well. Fear is like a lens or a great veil over the spirit and the true flow of the spirit is not released correctly because it gets distorted through the veil (of fear) that is in the soul. For this reason, the cleansing of bloodlines, the cleansing of mindsets, the alignment of letting the spirit guide your understanding, is so crucial.

"The soul is made to work in the 3-D realm. It is not made to work in spiritual matters and seeing matters. However, there is plenty of help for you—the angels, cloud of witnesses, Holy Spirit, Jesus, the Father; all these voices help you see all these things, to experience all these things, to encounter not from your soul realm, but from your spirit realm. This is for every believer who chooses walking into the discovery of this relationship." Mitchell smiled and said, "I will tell you this. In this hour, there are scales falling off many eyes."

Chapter 6

The Heavens are Open

John the Baptist preached the message "The Kingdom of Heaven is at hand" to the audiences gathered along the banks of the Jordan River where he then baptized the converts. He was saying more than we realize as he preached that message. The Passion Translation cites Matthew 3:2 in this manner:

> "The realm of Heaven's kingdom is about to appear," (TPT)

or

> "The kingdom realm of Heaven is about to appear." (TPT)

In Matthew 3, we find the story of John preaching that message when, one day, a relative arrives at the scene—his cousin Jesus. Only six months younger than John, Jesus had come to be baptized by John in the River Jordan. Initially, John refused to baptize Him, but Jesus convinced him that it must be done in order to fulfill all righteousness.[13]

Righteousness is often defined as "right standing with God." The ultimate right standing with God had not been in existence since the Garden of Eden. In the Garden, Adam and Eve co-existed with God, who would come down in the cool of the day and commune with them. Adam and Eve forfeited this privilege when they partook of the fruit from the Tree of the Knowledge of Good and Evil. Once their sin was exposed, God had no choice but to banish them from His presence. Covered in fig leaves, they were expelled from the Garden and an angel guardian kept them from returning and eating of the Tree of Life.

What was lost that day in the Garden was immediate access to the Father. It was not the Father's desire to lose fellowship and relationship with His creation, but through the deception of the serpent, it happened. After thousands of years, the long-term loss of fellowship and immediate access to God is about to end.

Look at the timeline and the balance of the story in the last half of Matthew chapter 3. It was revealed to John that Jesus would baptize in Holy Spirit, which was an entirely new dynamic that was barely even hinted at in Old Testament writings, but what John had been preaching was about to take on a whole new meaning. Let's read the story:

---

[13] Matthew 3:15

Then Jesus came from Galilee to John at the Jordan to be baptized by him. ¹⁴ And John tried to prevent Him, saying, "I need to be baptized by You, and are You coming to me?" ¹⁵ But Jesus answered and said to him, "Permit it to be so now, for thus it is fitting for us to fulfill all righteousness." Then he allowed Him.

¹⁶ When He had been baptized, Jesus came up immediately from the water; and behold, the heavens were opened to Him, and He saw the Spirit of God descending like a dove and alighting upon Him. ¹⁷ And suddenly a voice came from heaven, saying, "This is My beloved Son, in whom I am well pleased." (Matthew 3:13-17)

*¹⁶ And as ʳ Jesus rose up out of the water, **the heavenly realm opened up over him** and he saw the Holy Spirit descend out of the heavens and rest upon him in the form of a dove. ¹⁷ Then suddenly the voice of the Father shouted from the sky, saying, "This is the Son I love, and my greatest delight is in him." (TPT) (Emphasis mine)*

The dynamic being released into the earth at this time was the opening of the Heavens. Except on rare occasions, the heavens had not been opened to mankind since the Garden. Two immediate results of an open Heaven were evidenced: they saw and they heard!

> *When the Heavens are opened*
> *over your life, you will be able*
> *to see and hear from Heaven!*

The dove alighted upon Jesus and a voice came from Heaven. This voice from Heaven would be heard a couple of more times in Jesus' ministry time on the earth, but this was the first time and Jesus had not yet begun His ministry.

Notice what was said in verse 17:

> *17 And suddenly a voice came from heaven, saying, "This is My beloved Son, in whom I am well pleased."*

What was the Father so pleased about? Jesus had not yet begun His ministry. He had not healed anyone that we know of. He had not cast out any demons. He had not opened blind eyes or raised anyone from the dead. What was the Father so pleased about?

I propose to you that it was at least two-fold. In Jewish tradition, when a son had gone through the necessary apprenticeship and learned the trade of his father and had come to a point in time when he would be fully validated, the son could now operate the father's business as if it were his own. This occurred in the thirtieth year of the young man's life. He went from being a *"teknon"* to a "*uihos*"[14] son of his father. He was fully trained and fully capable of being about his father's business.

Becoming a Son

Many of us are familiar with the bar-mitzvah tradition of the Jews when, at twelve years of age, the young boy becomes a man, but this is a less familiar tradition of the Jews. In this tradition, the young man is now fully vested in his father's business and can operate with the same authority as the father himself. Anything the father could do, the son is now authorized to do in his stead. We have often wondered why Jesus waited until he was thirty years of age to begin his ministry. *Uihos* is the word used in verse 17.

In John 1:12 we find the use of the word *teknon* regarding becoming sons (or children) of God, simply upon receiving Jesus as savior. To become a *uihos* son requires some growth in our walk with God.

The second aspect on which I wish to focus is that access to God had begun to be fully restored. What had been lost for 4,000 years was coming to a swift close and the process of the restoration of open Heavens was now underway. It was initiated by this one event.

John's message that the Kingdom of Heaven is "at hand" might be better understood by a simple rephrasing: 'The Kingdom of Heaven is as close as your hand.' The

---

[14] Pronounced "wee-oss"

distinction is helpful, for, as we know, religion always seeks to make it hard to access Heaven. Religion has always come up with rules and more rules, hoops we must jump through, barriers we must cross—all in order to obtain Heaven. Jesus, however, was quite adept at removing barriers to Heaven, to God, to healing, and the like. If we understand that Heaven is not some far-away place—a future destination reserved for the remnant— but rather the abiding place of His Glory, we will find that we too can access this realm of existence—this dimension. It is not so far away as religion has tried to make it seem.

Heaven is closer than we think!

Following Jesus' baptism, Matthew records that Jesus began preaching around Galilee. The Passion Translation points out that the message John the Baptist preached was now being presented in the present tense:

> [17] *From that time on Jesus began to proclaim his message with these words: "Keep turning away from your sins and come back to God, **for heaven's kingdom realm is now accessible."** (Matthew 3:17 TPT) (Emphasis mine)*

Whereas for John the Baptist, the Kingdom was in the future, but once Jesus was baptized in the River Jordan, it became present/future tense.

The Heavens are open now!

In the next chapter, "Accessing the Realms of Heaven," I will talk about the simple process we utilize to help people access the realms of Heaven. God has made it quite simple and we have seen it be used effectively in thousands of lives to bring renewed hope, freshness, and blessing to people.

Chapter 7

Accessing the Realms of Heaven

A tremendous privilege we share in this time in history is the ability to access the realms of Heaven with ease. Many of us were taught that Heaven is only for after you die. Instead, Heaven is much more than a final destination on a journey; it can also be a vital aspect of that journey.

What I am about to share is vital for progressing in the various Courts of Heaven. We can access the Mercy Court while firmly planted here on the earth, but to maximize our endeavors in the Courts of Heaven, we need to learn how to operate FROM Heaven.

When teaching on accessing the realms of Heaven, I often point out some simple facts. If you were to tell me you were a citizen of a particular town, but you could tell me little of it from your personal experience, I would have a tendency to doubt the authenticity of your citizenship. I am a citizen of a small town in central North Carolina. I am familiar with the location of the city hall, police station, hospital, local county courthouse, Sheriff's Department and much more. I know where many sporting events will be held. I know where the parks are. I know many of the stores and restaurants. I am familiar with this small town. Yet, if I were to ask the average believer what they can describe of Heaven from personal experience, the answer would likely be, "Nothing". They have no personal experience of Heaven that they can relate to me. It does not have to be like that.

In Matthew 3, Jesus informed us that the Kingdom of Heaven was at hand. Again, we could say, "the Kingdom of Heaven is as close as your hand." Hold your hand up in front of your nose as close as you can. Do not touch your nose. Heaven is closer to you than that. It is not far, far away up in the sky. It is not "over yonder" as some old hymns describe. It is a very present reality separated from us by a very thin membrane – and we can access it by faith. It is very simple.

When Jesus was baptized in the River Jordan, as he came up out of the water IMMEDIATELY the heavens were opened. He both saw (a dove) and heard (a voice coming from Heaven). This one act of Jesus restored our ability to access Heaven. We can experience open heavens over our life. We do not have to wait. We can live conscious of the realm of Heaven and live out of that reality!

Everything we do as believers we must do by faith. Accessing the realms of Heaven is done the same way. Prophetic acts can create realities for us, and it is the same with this. You can visualize stepping from one room into another easily. It is like stepping from one place to another. To learn to access the realms of Heaven, you will follow the same pattern.

Stand up from where you are now and prepare to work with me. You can experience the realms of Heaven right now! You do not have to wait until you are dressed up in a long box at the local funeral home or filling an urn. You can experience Heaven while you are alive! Remember, we enter the Kingdom as a child.

How to Access Heaven

Quiet yourself down. Turn off distracting background noises if possible. Prepare to relax and focus. Now, say this with me:

Father, I would like to access the realms of Heaven today, so right now, by faith I take a step into the realms of Heaven.

As you say that, close your eyes and take a step forward. As you step forward, imagine you are going from one place to another in a single step. Once you have done so, pay attention to what you see and hear. You may see very bright lights; you may see a river, a pastoral scene, a garden—any number of things. Right now, you are experiencing a taste of Heaven. You will notice the peace that pervades the atmosphere of Heaven. You might notice the air seems electric with life. The testimonies I have heard are always amazing and beautiful to hear.

Now spend a few minutes in this place. Remember, Jesus said that to enter the Kingdom you must come as a little child. I often coach people to imagine yourself as an 8-year-old seeing what you are seeing. What would an 8-year-old do? He or she would be inquisitive and ask, "What is this? What does that do? Where does that go? Can I go here?" If a child saw a river or a lake, what would that child want to do? Most would want to jump into the water.

The variety is infinite. The colors are amazing! The sounds are so beautiful. You can learn to do this on a regular basis. When you access the realms of Heaven, you are home. You were made to experience the beauty that is Heaven.

The reason learning to access the realms of Heaven is crucial to engaging the Courts of Heaven is that much of what we do needs to be done FROM Heaven. We need to learn to engage Heaven and work from that place.

Seeing versus Knowing

Many people tell me they cannot "see" visually in the spirit. Often, they are discounting the ability they do have. They may be discounting their "knower." Every believer has a "knower" at work within them. This "knower" who is Holy Spirit at work within you helps you perceive things. Whether something is good or evil, He works to guide you more than you may have realized. Most navy submarines have a device known as sonar. Sonar gives a submarine "eyes" to see what is in their vicinity. They can detect what the object is by the ping emitted by the sonar. They can determine the distance to the object and if it is another submarine. They can even identify what class of submarine it might be. Sonar is invaluable in this setting, but a video camera would be rather useless underwater.

The military has a similar device for above ground situations known as radar. It functions in much the same manner as the sonar. If a pilot were flying through thick cloud cover, the pilot would need to know what is in his path. Radar becomes his eyes.

Some people function visually. They often see what amounts to pictures or video images when they "see" in the spirit. They may see more detail. Yet one operating by his or her "knower" (their spiritual radar or sonar) can be just as effective as a seer. If you operate more like sonar or radar, do not discount what you "see" in that manner. It is how I function, and I have been doing this type of work for many years.

I can often detect where an angel is in the room (or if it is one of the men or women in white linen and not an angel). I can often detect how many are present and whether they have something they are to give to someone. I can detect any number of things and even though it is not "visual" it is still a form of "seeing." It will set your mind at ease when you understand that operating by your "knower" is just as valid as any other type of vision. It will help you to realize you have been seeing much more than you know and you may know much more than some who only see.

Factors Hindering Seeing or Hearing

When someone tells me they have trouble seeing or hearing in the realm of the spirit, I have found a common cause for much of the problem. Most of us have some measure of Freemasonry in our background. As part of the oaths and ceremonies of Freemasonry, one makes a covenant with their eyes to not be able to see spiritually. They symbolize this with the act of putting on the hoodwink (or blindfold) in the early initiation ceremonies. They are making a covenant to be spiritually blind. If they did not make this kind of covenant in the early stages of Freemasonry, they would be able to see the darkness they are getting themselves involved in.

The person needs to get the false verdicts empowering Freemasonry overturned in their lives. I recommend my book, *Overcoming the False Verdicts of Freemasonry*. I have found a correlation between Freemasonry and the inability to see or hear spiritually about 90% of the time.

The second situation I have found is the person who has made a covenant with their eyes not to see. Usually this is the result of having been frightened earlier in their life when they saw something spiritually. This can happen particularly with a small child who may see something in a dream or vision, and it frightens them so much that they shut down the seeing or hearing.

The resolution for this is to become willing to step back into the scene that frightened them, but this time, invite Jesus to be with them in the situation. When he shows up the fear seems to dissipate. I ask them to repent for shutting down the spiritual vision and/or hearing part of their life and have them ask Jesus to reopen their seeing or hearing.

The last situation we have recently discovered is that someone has gotten a false title, lien, note, or lease agreement that blocks the person's ability to see in the spirit or somehow the enemy has placed a tarpaulin (tarp[15]) over them to block seeing and hearing.

We step into the Court of Titles and Deeds and request that every false title of ownership or false note over our spiritual sight or hearing be dissolved and the ownership of the Lord Jehovah be established over our spiritual eyes and ears.

If it involves a lien against our ability to see or hear, we request that it be marked satisfied by the blood of Jesus. We forgive the person or persons involved in making the false claim of ownership, we bless them, and we release them.

If a lease agreement is involved, we also ask that the false lease agreement be cancelled, and a righteous ownership claim be established between the person and the Lord Jehovah.

We also request any tarpaulins (tarps) over their eyes and life be immediately removed. We have seen

---

[15] A large sheet placed to cover or protect objects. In the natural they are usually made of canvas or plastic.

immediate results when doing this as people's spiritual eyes are suddenly opened as well as their spiritual ears.

Chapter 8

Four Keys to Hearing God's Voice

D r. Mark Virkler has written extensively on this subject over the years. It is his signature teaching and has helped thousands of believers learn to hear and record what Heaven is saying to them on an ongoing basis. His website (cwgministries.org) has a myriad of materials to assist you in learning to do spirit-led journaling. I will simply summarize his teaching here because it is a vital discipline for you to learn to maximize Heaven down in your life.

Heaven wants to talk with you. The Father wants to be able to talk with you, as does Jesus and Holy Spirit. Heaven has even arranged it so that angels will talk with us. It happened numerous times in the Bible. Remember when Gabriel visited Mary and Joseph, the angels came to the shepherds in the field, and many other times when angels came. Not only did the angels come and speak to these people, but on several occasions, they had conversations with them. The people asked questions and received answers. Abraham conversed with men in white linen about the fate of Sodom and Gomorrah. Other instances of men in white appearing to humans is recorded. Men in white are saints that have already passed on from earth to Heaven. These beings can talk with you just as they did with Jesus on the Mount of Transfiguration (see Mark 9 and Matthew 17). If we find men in white, then it stands to reason that there are women in white linen also.

Some will argue that to speak with a man in white is to talk to the dead. If that is the case, Jesus was guilty of talking to the dead, but Heaven's perspective is different from our faulty earthly perspective. They are not considered dead by earthly standards. Their bodies may have ceased to live, but their spirit is quite alive in Heaven. Jesus did not consider them dead. He said in Matthew 22:32:

> 'I am the God of Abraham, the God of Isaac, and the God of Jacob. God is not the God of the dead, but of the living."

Jesus spoke this when He was upon the earth and these three men had long since transitioned from the earth to Heaven. As a matter of fact, Jesus foretold that we would be able to sit down with men such as these in the Kingdom of Heaven.

> And I say to you that many will come from east and west, and sit down with Abraham, Isaac, and Jacob in the kingdom of heaven. (Matthew 8:11)

Remember, the Kingdom of Heaven is at hand—it is as close as your hand. It is not far away.

Get Ready

Now, before we begin, get some paper to write on or prepare your computer to type into. Get a pen or pencil with which to write that is in working order. Instruct your soul to back up and call your spirit to come forward. Once you are aware this has happened, you are ready to proceed.

Step 1: Quiet Yourself

The first principle to learn is to quiet yourself down so that you can hear your spirit within you and hear Holy Spirit within you. This will probably require you to turn off the TV or any music you have playing and simply get quiet.

Once you have learned to quiet yourself by shutting out all the distractions around you, you will be able to do this anywhere you go. I can do this in a noisy sports event because I have learned to quiet myself.

Step 2: Look to Jesus

You are not looking to anyone else, you are looking to Jesus. You are going to do what the writer of Hebrews 12:2 said to do: "Look unto Jesus." You do not have to fear other voices getting involved here. You have a promise from your heavenly Father that if you ask Him for something, He will provide it. You are not asking Satan or his demons to speak to you. They are not permitted to. When I practice this, they are not invited to speak, and I will tell them so. You can do the same.

Step 3: Tune to Flow

Now with your eyes fixed on Jesus, you are ready for the next step. It is time to tune into the flow of Holy Spirit within you. Holy Spirit flows within you like a river would flow down a mountainside. As a matter of fact, John recorded in John 7:38 that rivers of living water would flow from within. You are simply recognizing the current that is flowing. Within that current are messages from Heaven that you can tune to like you would turn the tuning knob on a radio to pick up a particular radio station. As you tune to the flow from Heaven, you will begin the next step.

Step 4: Write it Down

What Heaven has to say is important and you need to write down what you are hearing. At this point, do not try to analyze what you are hearing; simply record what you are hearing. You can analyze it later. Begin to write what you hear. Do not focus on writing it in a nice pretty style; simply write. You can fix it later.

It is my long-time practice to simply ask this question:

What does Heaven have to say to me today?

By phrasing my question in that manner, I am opening myself to hear from the Father, if He is the one speaking, or Jesus, should He choose to speak on that occasion, or

Holy Spirit, who I will hear from often, but I am also open to whomever Heaven chooses to speak to me. Just as the Old Testament prophets experienced, sometimes they received messages from angels or from men in white linen. I simply want to hear from Heaven, and I leave it to their discretion to have whomever they choose to speak to me. I can rest in the fact that they will not be speaking to me something that is contrary to the Word of God or what the Father, Son, or Holy Spirit might speak.

What Heaven has to say will always bless. It will always encourage, always comfort, always bring peace. Remember, I told you not to analyze what you heard while you are writing because you can do that later. Once you have heard and recorded all that Heaven has to say at that time, you can then review it and clarify anything you thought you heard. I typically type my journaling for a couple of reasons. 1) I have a record of it that I can find and review fairly easily by using the search features in my computer. 2) My typing is a lot easier to read than my handwriting. 3) I can type for a lot longer than I can write by hand.

Donna prefers to write her journaling in a journal book. She will use different colors of ink to help her distinguish between journaling, recording a dream or vision, or other types of instruction. The main thing is to write down what Heaven is saying. I cannot contend in prayer for what I have forgotten. If I have a record, I can recall it and contend in prayer for that particular thing.

An important thing to remember when first learning to journal from your spirit is to not ask questions that are too involved. You do not need a detailed description of the seven horses of the apocalypse from Revelation. Do not start with something like that. Keep it simple.

You are judging based on the sense of "Was this from Heaven or not?" Remember, the Comforter (Holy Spirit) will comfort, however, the condemner (Satan) will condemn. The Peace-giver gives peace while the destroyer destroys. Heaven will give good reports. You do not have to fear Heaven saying bad things to you. They will on occasion correct me on something, but because I am a son, I understand that correction keeps me safe. If I do not want correction, am I really a son?

When you are first learning to journal, you may ask a trusted friend to help you ascertain "Was this Heaven or not?" You are not asking them to judge the content, just the flavor of it. You may also, at this point, make any spelling corrections or possibly even recopy what you heard in a clearer manner. Sometimes when journaling by hand, you may drift off the lines or run to the edge of the paper. That will not bother some people, but others want to have their work look much nicer.

If you are having trouble tuning to the flow, pause and begin to pray in the spirit for a few moments. That may be helpful for you in the process.

I have also found it helpful to have my time with the Lord in journaling be the first thing I do in the morning before checking emails or engaging in a lot of conversation. You may find the same thing works best for you. For others, the end of the day works for you. Whatever works. I encourage you to make this a daily practice. Some days you will hear a lot, while on other days, just a few things may be spoken. I have experienced days when I typed several pages of material and on other days, very little was spoken at that time. Simply adjust to the flow of Heaven.

Let us review the four keys:

1. **Quiet Yourself** – Learn to quiet yourself so you can tune into Heaven.
2. **Look Unto Jesus** – we are not looking for anyone outside of Heaven to be speaking to us—they are not invited to the party!
3. **Tune to the Flow of the Spirit Within** – The Holy Spirit flows through our spirit like a river. We can learn to tune to the flow and hear what Heaven is saying.
4. **Write it Down!** Begin to record what you are hearing or perceiving. YOU can judge it when you are finished listening for Heaven. Do not concern yourself with how it looks on the page. Simply record it—whether handwritten, drawn, or typed, make a record of it!

At CourtsNet.com you will find our video course to help you in this process.

Chapter 9

The Tool of the Prayer Language

In the wisdom of God, He provided many tools for believers to enhance their walk with God and improve the quality of their lives. One of the most vital of these tools is the ability to pray from *your* spirit realm in a language you never learned. It is a means of communication for *your* spirit to connect directly with Heaven. If you need to pray and do not have the words or the insight into how to pray, your spirit is able to communicate accurately with Heaven concerning the need. That is a wonderful tool to have at our disposal.

By utilizing our ability to pray in our prayer language, we are able to stir up our spirit realm. In the process, our mind will be quickened, and our soul will be quickened to cooperate with Holy Spirit working in our lives. At times, we can pray in our prayer language and it will be like stirring up a container that has been still for a period of time. It will stir our spirit and cause it to feel refreshed.

Not only can we pray in this way, but we can also sing from our spirit. Our spirit hears and understands the melodies of Heaven and can join in with what Heaven is singing or saying at any given time. If you have experienced singing in the spirit, simply release your spirit to make melody to the Lord. You will be refreshed by the beauty of the experience.

Sometimes when journaling, I will pray a few moments in my prayer language and it will "jump start" my ability to hear more clearly and journal more effectively. You may find it helpful to do that as well.

What I am referring to has also been called "speaking in tongues," which refers to a person speaking from their spirit in a language they never learned. The devil has sought to malign speaking in tongues and has induced people to mock what they did not understand, but their mockery in no way lessens the validity of praying in a language outside of our mental understandings, nor does it lessen the value of it.

The strategy of the enemy has always been to discredit what he could not control. He has done the same with speaking in tongues because he fears the potential of it against his realm. The release to a believer to pray in a language unknown to them is the result of receiving the Baptism in the Holy Spirit. When we are born again, we are baptized BY Holy Spirit into the Body of Christ.[16] As a result, Holy Spirit indwells our spirit realm and lives

---

[16] 1 Corinthians 12:13

within us. At some point afterward, we should have been baptized in water by a fellow believer—often a pastor or apostle. Yet another baptism taught in the Bible is called the Baptism *in* the Holy Spirit. Jesus is the one who baptizes the believer *into* the Holy Spirit.[17] It is a way to experience Holy Spirit in an even more intimate manner. As a believer, Holy Spirit is *IN you*, but you are not *IN Him* unless you have been baptized in the Holy Spirit. To be baptized in the Holy Spirit is to be immersed into His nature, power, characteristics, and more. Some of the results are that Jesus will become even more real to you, you will find deeper intimacy in your times of prayer and fellowship with Heaven, you will experience more boldness in witnessing of Jesus, and you will be able to pray directly from your spirit, bypassing your mind. You will also be able to worship more intimately by singing from your spirit. These are just some of the many benefits of the Baptism in the Holy Spirit.

In the last chapter of the book of Mark, the writer prophesies that "they shall speak with new tongues." In Acts 2, on the Day of Pentecost, the 120 people gathered in the upper room collectively experienced this phenomenon. It was so distinct that those who heard these believers heard them speak in languages that could be understood by some of the listeners as their native language, even those the speakers had never learned their language. What were they speaking? The praises of God

---

[17] Luke 3:16

according to Acts 2:11. It was a sign and wonder to those who witnessed it.

Isaiah prophesied about this centuries before, as he indicated one of the benefits of praying in the spirit, which is to help you experience rest in your soul.[18]

In a number of places in the book of Acts, this phenomenon appeared. In some cases, with the believers' initial experience of receiving the Baptism in the Holy Spirit, they not only spoke in tongues but also prophesied. Paul gave instructions concerning the orderly use of this ability in public settings in 1 Corinthians 14. Paul encouraged speaking in tongues, indicating he knew the value of it. He also instructed the Thessalonians to not forbid the speaking in tongues.

If you have yet to experience this, simply ask Jesus to baptize you in the Holy Spirit, yield yourself to speak the words that bubble up within you and say them aloud. It does not have to be fluent initially—that will come. Merely enjoy the presence of the Lord in this moment. The Holy Spirit will not *make* you speak in tongues. He will give you the syllables to speak but you will have to give voice to those syllables. You will have to let the words or phrases come forth. You just need to turn up the volume so that your ears can hear it and go for it!

---

[18] Isaiah 28:11

Chapter 10

Deeding Territories

Donna was talking to a group of friends recently and was discussing the imagination. People do not realize that the imagination is God-given. You have one imagination, but there are two parts of you that can use it—your soul can use it, or your spirit can use it. It is like a canvas. Your soul can paint on it your hopes and dreams, or your spirit can paint what is going on in the Kingdom of Heaven. It is just one canvas, but the content on it and the source of the content depends on which part of you is using it.

This canvas, however, is also transparent. Think of it like a window. It can be utilized from the soul side or the spirit side, or even a little of both. When we talk about tapping into the realms of Heaven or engaging with angels or men and women in white linen, then we are letting the Spirit of God, through our oneness with our own spirit, use the same canvas of imagination. It is like a window in that you can look *through* it or you can look *past* it.

In some ways, I think you could think of it like a hologram. Something is projected upon it. It looks like it is present with you, but it is not. This is how you engage the realms of Heaven through the sanctified imagination. Once Jesus holds the territory and the title deed, the all-important title deed, if any squatter or demonic thing tries to land, you can easily get angels to help to kick them out, to bind them, or to reveal your title—the title of Jesus to that realm—and command that the trespassers leave.

This seems to make things easier along the way. After you have had the title deed of your imagination given over to Jesus, you must realize that your imagination is neutral. It is not evil and is not righteous. It is neutral and it resides in you and it becomes a tool for you. Some can make it evil because they are devising evil plans that use the soul realm imagination. Some evil entities are coming, and they are using it without your knowing of it and they are devising their evil plans on that place of your imagination—that inner screen and that is for evil. You must stop that. You are the only one that should shut that down because you are the original owner of your own imagination. God designed it for you, but when you become born again, you can surrender that and give it the title deed to that territory within your realm to Jesus for His use for righteousness sake. Then, should any ugly, evil, wicked thing attempt to use that your imagination, just simply say "I am calling in the host of Heaven to kick you out of the territory that belongs to the Lord. Get out of here in Jesus' name." The balance of this chapter is on how to deed the territory of your imagination to the Lord.

Donna began to share another story. For a couple of years, she had been meditating on the word throne. "We have been taught that in Heaven the Father has His throne and Satan wants the Father's throne and he wants to put his throne higher than God's throne, but God is El Elyon and He is the Highest Throne. When sons and daughters begin realizing that if I am made in His likeness, then the Father gave me a throne in my realm. This was before I had the word realm, but the hope of Heaven would be that I would remove self from my realms throne and invite Jesus to take that throne. He would then have kingship over my realm," she explained.

Sanctified Imagination

One morning, Donna was having a moment in the presence of the Lord. She felt like she had already given her throne to Jesus, but an area in her realm existed (because now she had different language for the concept) that needed to be addressed. Earlier in her walk with the Lord, she began using the phrase 'sanctified imagination,' and so she said, "I am going to sanctify my imagination."

Removing the Squatters

She asked the Lord, "Lord, would you kick out Satan? If any darkened parts of my imagination exist that he is squatting on, then he is an illegal squatter because I am a child of God, so in the courts, I ask you to remove every squatter on the grounds that I have been purchased by God, through His own blood and His inner body."

She told the Lord, "I want to trade with you every unsanctified imagination, that I might have a complete and whole sanctified imagination, so that from today forward, I only operate only out of that with no tainting. What does that look like? How do I receive that?"

As soon as she said that, she saw into her realm and saw the King of Glory had come in.[19] She saw that she had removed herself from the throne and asked Jesus to sit on the throne. She saw the Father sitting on it, the Son sitting on it, and the Holy Spirit sitting on it. Then she saw a long line of people, like a retinue of people who travel with a king. They wanted to come into her realm and all of them had the name of a quality of Yahweh. She saw wisdom, purity, righteousness, glory, and peace, among others. As she saw each of these beings, she began to say, "I invite you in my realm. I want you to be comfortable here. I want you to be at home here, and I want you to stay here." Then she asked her angels to make sure that all of those coming into her realm knew they were welcomed. She charged her angels to keep the gate open, to allow them entrance, and to welcome them in.

As she was doing that, she had a funny feeling that, if something in her realm was not needful, if she did not tell it to leave, then more of the heavenly beings could not come in. It is like where you are cleaning out the garage

---

[19] Psalm 24:7-10

and you have to get rid of the old stuff so that you can organize what you have in order to make room for new stuff.

She began to ask the Lord, "What am I hanging on to?" And He said, "This is what you asked me about—this release of the old imagination, the release of the unsanctified imagination."

She said, "In Jesus' name, I command every unsanctified imagination in me to leave now." It was as if she could see them leave through a gate. She watched many things leave and they appeared like beings, but she never saw a called "Sanctified Imagination" come into her realm. She asked, "Is that part of my realm or is there something to do?"

Deeding Your Imagination

As soon as she said that, she was in a courtroom in the Court of Titles and Deeds. The counsel of the court was saying to her, "What you need to do is deed over your imagination to the King of Glory." She realized she had never made a legal trade in the Courts of Heaven that deeded the territory called Imagination in her realm to Jesus. The territory of her imagination was still legally in her name. There was a document in the Court of Titles and Deeds that represented that territory. It represented who had the right of ownership to it, and she still held the deed. She could see on the document where the enemy had made inroads and he had previously had pieces of it. He did not have pieces of it anymore, so he was not the owner. It did not say "Satan," or "King of Darkness"—it did not say anything like that, but she knew that she held it and she was at a tipping point where she was on the precipice of a decision.

Another Scenario of Deeding the Territory

Shortly after working with Donna's situation of Deeding the Territory of her imagination, we did a similar thing with someone else. It had a couple of different nuances that you may need to consider for yourself or someone you are working with.

In the Court of Titles and Deeds we presented our case:

Jesus, I deed this territory of my imagination over to you. I do it freely. I do not want to be the deed owner. I do not want to have an ownership of my imagination; I want you to have ownership of my imagination. Would you, by this court, come and take ownership, full occupancy, and own the deed of my imagination and thereby sanctify it?

We were asked by the Court, "Do you do this with your full intent and choice of desire?"

"Yes," we replied.

We also asked the court for eviction papers for the removal of all squatters, which would be all forms of darkness because we are a child of God, purchased by Him.

We continued:

In my realm, I have put Jesus on His throne, but there are still squatters on my imagination, so I'm taking the deed of my imagination and I request this documentation in the Court of Titles and Deeds for the removal of every squatter who has illegally been occupying territory in my imagination.

When that paperwork got done, we could feel that the squatters had been removed. It was instantaneous. We felt we now had a free and clear deed, but we did not want to own it; we wanted Jesus to own it. That is when we asked for a deed transfer and we signed it over by our intent and made our request to the King and asked that He would become the titled owner of the deed of our imagination. At that point, we saw Jesus' name on the signature line of the deed.

This is essentially our request to the court:

I request access to the Court of Titles and Deeds. I request eviction papers for every squatter of whatever realm, place, or time, upon the territory of my imagination. I choose today, by an act of my will, to transfer ownership of my imagination to the Father, Son, and Holy Spirit.

Once the request was granted, Lydia indicated that the court would document this action in their records and that this provides us with a door of entry for the King of

Glory,[20] so all that is left to do is to ask that the door be opened, in order for the King of Glory to come into the territory of your imagination and sanctify it fully in every respect.

> *I request that the gate of my imagination be opened so the King of Glory might come in and sanctify the territory of my imagination fully and possess it as His territory.*
>
> *King of Glory, enter in through the new door into your territory. I have deeded this territory to you from the Court of Titles and Deeds. Possess this fully with Your Glory. Thank you, Lord.*

Lydia then said, "Now declare you have a sanctified imagination."

"I have a sanctified imagination," I declared.

Synchronizing Your Clock

Because you have done the prior work, often your life has been out of synchronization with the timing of the Lord. To get that corrected, you will need to access the Court of Times and Seasons and request your clock be synchronized with this amendment entitled "As If It Never Were."

---

[20] Psalm 24

In Jesus' name, I request access to the Court of Times and Seasons.

Based on the documentation that I received regarding the transfer of the title deed of my imagination to the Lord of hosts, to Holy Spirit and to Jesus, and the eviction of all squatters who illegally held places in my imagination, and the event of the opening of the door to my realm to the King of Glory and his possession of my imagination—based on all of this, I request in the Court of Times and Seasons that my clock and seasons be synchronized to as if it never were.

At that point, a court assistant took the paperwork and we began to hear gongs on my clock. The clock was at one o'clock and the angels moved it back to 12 noon and were letting it cycle through its timing. Your experience may vary from our experience. A settling of peace will accompany the completion of the work in this court.

The Amendment of "As If It Never Were" does exactly what the name says. It resets your life (spiritually) to how it would be, had the intervening events never happened.

Once Donna had completed the court work in the Court of Titles and Deeds, she could sense a lot of talking in the court. Suddenly she could the name Jesus written on the bottom of the deed where her name had been moments before.

As soon as she said aloud what she saw, a flooding of peace filled her realm. She realized quite quickly that the being called Peace now made a larger home in her realm. Peace could expand in her realm and fill more of the space. Peace occupied more space because Donna had made a choice to name the King as the deed owner of her imagination.

"It just began to feel so right, like dominoes in a line that all go down," Donna described. "It was like everything began to click in line." This is what a sanctified imagination and transferring ownership of the deed by choice (because the Father has left it to our choice) over to the Father, Son, and Holy Spirit does. Notice, the Lord does not make claim on it—because that is controlling and manipulative—but the Father grants us the deed until we desire to give it to the King.

Lydia explained, "The Transfer of Title, in the case of the imagination, benefits the son or daughter of God with the mind of Christ and a pure flow of sanctified imagination. Imagination is so highly sought after in your world because it is the first step of entrance into things beyond the 3-D realm, the natural plane, and is given to humans specifically for a first step into places beyond their physical sight and physical senses.

"For example, animals in the 3-D realm do not have imagination. Theirs is replaced with instinct. As you learn about realms and the need of your realm to be filled with the righteousness of God, He will point out a territory within your realm (if you have given Him the throne) that does not bow or acquiesce to the throne that you have given Him. That is an area He is not ruling over within you.

"In this instance, it was the imagination. Because you have deeded the territory to a new owner, the King—who you have installed on the throne of your realm by your desire—He has access to benefit you with all the original design that He made the imagination for.

"Now, Satan is doing the same thing on the other side. He is tricking people, deceiving them, and gaining and capturing the territories of their imagination. His sole purpose is to bring about more evil into the world through deception, lies, manipulation, and bondages."

It is vital for our spirit-led life that we deed the ownership of every territory we possess over to the Lord of Hosts, to Jesus, His Son, and to Holy Spirit. Territories most of us, if not all of us, possess include:

- Territory of our Imagination
- Territory of our Relationships
- Territory of our Finances
- Territory of our Intellect
- Territory of our Physical Body
- Territory of our Sexuality
- Territory of our Work Life

These are just some of the many territories that comprise us. As we yield ownership and lordship over from ourselves to the Lord of Hosts, Jesus, and Holy Spirit, we will experience life with them in a fresh new way. Enjoy your journey.

Chapter 11

Becoming a Revelation Receiver

It was during yet another meeting with Heaven when Lydia spoke, "Envision a chess board where the King of kings has won the game and you get to remind the enemy that the match has already been won. It is a check mate, for God's Kingdom reigns supreme over every lesser kingdom, and every deity pretending to call itself God. However, the need for the saints to recognize their role as children of God to agree with His will in the earth realm so that the plans of God can continue to unfold in planet earth and cause it to triumph in full measure and in every area with finality and completeness is great is crucial. The plans the Father has for His church, as well as the plans He has for His people, and the fact that He must announce the greatness of who He is to the earth, are all present.

The children of God are engaged in the working out of these plans.

These plans include freeing captives (those held in captivity to spiritual bondages) and these plans are also linked to their freedom through God's sons and daughters. We get to participate!

"Confrontation with the world and its systems and structures is unavoidable, but do not be frightened, weak, or feel vulnerable to the systems of this world because the greater Kingdom is coming closer, and as it approaches in closer dimensions, the enemy is more wrathful, and the battle is more easily seen," Lydia continued. "This plays into the purposes and plans of the godhead and even of the church. The ecclesias of the earth are beginning to see the warfare more clearly. *This should not frighten you; this should enlighten you* to your part and your place, even your position in Christ Jesus as overcomers. You have already secured the triumph.

"New revelation of God's people's role and position in this victory is being released. You must have awareness of the war in spiritual places and allow it to motivate you to your position and role as a son of God, one who operates in assurance of the Father's business, His activity, and His plan.

"Many things are being uncovered to your sight. Even now, do not let the uncovering of evil frighten you.

Have no agreement with fear.

"Allow the work with the angels of God as they uncover the bold contradictions of the enemy's lies and shenanigans to cause your spirit to rejoice because you have knowledge of the one who overcomes all in seeking God for knowledge.

Request angelic activity to work
with the words of your mouth
as you release this knowledge
into different realms.

"This refers to angelic realms, human realms, physical plane realms, and spiritual realms. The sons and daughters of God are beginning to see who they really are. They are beginning to know the triumphant power of God that dwells richly within them as they release it verbally, as they do this without religious thought but as a family member of God's family, born again through the blood and cross of Jesus.

"As you do this, your mind begins to shift to authority, and you begin to see with wider acceptance your own ability of agreement and alignment with the godhead to enforce the victory of Jesus.

"Surely this is a calling up of the armies of the church, and here I do not mean the angelic armies—I mean the armies of God's children who sometimes war, and sometimes release the angels to war, and sometimes operate in more kingly dispensations of the release of a Word of God. Please know this," Lydia implored. "Angels are on assignment to hear what the saints are saying.

> *Please understand the words of the saints must match the words of the Father for angels to go to work.*

"I am talking about what you have as written word, but I am also talking about what you have as supernatural word, the rhema word, the breath of Yahweh. I also mean the spirit leading your ears and eyes to know that an unfolding needs to happen, and the Father has decided, of His will, that He will work with His sons and daughters in the earth so that His will would be done in the earth," she concluded.

Revelation Helps Thwart the Enemy

We asked Lydia, "How does this work out against the plans of the enemy?"

She responded, "You can supernaturally understand the plans of the enemy so that you can circumvent them. After all, are you not from a more powerful kingdom?

> *Revelation sometimes appears to your sight as to what the plans of wickedness would accomplish for the express purpose of you bringing about the plans of God in that circumstance.*

"You have learned this must be done in numerous ways: court cases, declarations, agreements, and verbal releasing of that agreement, so that the angelic activity around you hearkens to that word.

Releasing Rhemas

"The Word of God—and I am not talking about scriptures but talking about rhema[21]—

The Word of God released from your tongue Is exactly what angels listen for and they go to work.

"This was the powerful moment of the amazement of Jesus when He talked to the Centurion because He saw the Centurion understood.

What is in the unseen spiritual realm can be seen, known, heard, picked up, and understood by God's children maturing as they will.
Some choose not to mature.

"Heaven has no issue with that because Heaven trusts the Spirit to do His work of revelation, so that your minds

---

[21] Rhema is the Greek word describing a word that has become alive to you.

can begin to understand the role of the saved in the earth realm.

"For too many seasons, the church—and I do not mean church like you would define it in the past, I mean the praying ecclesias—have been shy of their true authority and ability.

> *Remember, there is great power*
> *in where two or more agree and touch*
> *upon the same thing,*
> *asking of the Father to release*
> *His power to that thing.*

"Many in your day are awakening to this and must continue to awaken to it.

"Not only do we have Scribe Angels, which have been sent out into the earth to record the words of the saints as they verbally release the Word of God, but there are other angels who have been released to *prompt the saints to release the Word of God,*" Lydia explained. "Many among you are leaders in this while some are just coming into it.

> *What must be understood is the work*
> *of darkness to cloak the verbal words*
> *of God's saints.*

"Words are warfare. They end wars, begin wars, and settle wars. It has always been a clash of kingdoms. However, from our viewpoint, this clash of kingdoms is only to grow up the saints to reveal to them their true position in Christ and the overcoming victory of His kingdom." she clarified.

Becoming a Revelation Receiver

Be encouraged that new revelation can come to those who ask, seek, and hunger as if a starved man at a banquet for the revelation that Yahweh wants them to release over their spheres of influence.

Remember, each sphere of influence has a boundary as apportioned to them by God.

Are you filling up your boundary with the words of God?

Are you asking angels to assist you in the receipt of revelation?

Do you know the revelatory Word of God over a circumstance in your sphere?

Some of this is plainly evidenced in scripture. The Lord has not left us unknowing, but in our day—in our current calendar on earth—we must receive the Word of the Lord by revelation, by dreams and visions, and by understanding all of this through the lens of the goodness of God. He wants to grow up His children. His plan is for the righteousness within His children to be seen. The people who are listening to this ministry are seeking to be these mouths in the earth. Some, if not most, are hidden in private and do this in their prayer work, which causes Heaven to rejoice.

"An army has been mobilized among God's people and any who desire to join shall do so simply by faith—through what they release as the revelatory Word of God, not agreeing with the presentation of world structures, but agreeing with truth through the Spirit of Truth and through the opening of the ear. That is the work of angels in this area," Lydia explained. "Is it not great fun?

"I am using the word *fun* to refer to when you see the outcome of a contended timeline as it settles through the verbal release of the ecclesia in agreement with the will and purposes of God. Is it not a moment of joy where you see this take place through agreements within the Body of Christ on earth?

Your Common Goal

Unity and a sense of oneness comes from laboring together for common goals.

"Let your common goal be what is written in scripture and what is revealed to you. Make room for different expressions of the same goals of heavenly places and give room to those among you who are empowered by the Spirit to fulfill their mission in this hour. Your great joy comes from this as you see enemy plots exposed and defeated. Do not worry about the timeframe. Leave the timing of it to the heavenly realm—to the unseen realm and the activity of the angels. Believe me, they are at work," Lydia advised. "You are going to be able to sense their work in greater measure in future days. Let this cause your heart to rejoice."

She continued, "It is possible to rejoice in advance of the manifestation of the result in the 3-D realm. Your spirit knows how to do this. **Give permission to your spirit to come forth and rejoice in the victory of the Lord in all circumstances.** This will preserve your soul and keep it from weariness.

Focus on the things of the Lord.

"Divide out—and you can request angels to help you with this—and discern the frequencies of the Lord and the activities of angels versus that of darkness. Your spirit can help you do this.

The Power of Silence

"Let me give you a reminder of how powerful your words truly are," Lydia continued. "Be mindful to steward and shepherd over your words well—not from the soulish realm as some do, but from your spirit. Silence—and what I mean by that is what we call holding our tongue or not making an expression of sound—is as important as what you agree with vocally. Silence is a symbol of disagreement.

What you do not vocalize is equally important as what you do vocalize.

"It is as if I give you permission not to say anything. You will see this in scripture where it is told of Jesus who as the lamb before the slaughter, He did not open His mouth.[22] This is a sign of trusting the Lord. Some try to battle verbally with other humans when the skirmish is not in the natural plane, it is in the unseen plane. You must address this plane before the natural plane can align to carry the weight of the truth you must release.

"Are these not good mysteries?" Lydia asked us.

"I encourage you that this is just some of the foundational things we as children of God get to be reminded of.

A Symbol of Strategy

Lydia continued, "Remember, I started this by talking about a chess board. The chess board is a symbol of strategy. You need to recall how strategic (this is the word you use) your Father in Heaven truly is. He is so strategic that He laughs from His throne at the antics of a defeated kingdom for He has won His children back to Himself by

---

[22] Isaiah 53:7, Matthew 17:27

His own son and the blood that He shed. He is not worried, and He has great plans for earth's realm even still.

Rejoice!

"Worship is rejoicing, so set your mind to rejoicing. The battle has an outcome of victory, but the strategies in play as on a chess board sometimes are not seen until the final move. I share this symbol with you that you may know you are involved in a strategic time and that YOU are strategic," she clarified. "Your position is strategic to what the Father is doing as you learn who you are and begin to rest in the truth of what He is calling each person to do. Personal assignments, even small ones, are great in His sight.

Work with the Angels

"Work with the angels of God, receive their messages. Some of these messages will be brought in dreams. Some will be brought in knowings. Begin to trust this. However, I will say this. The work of this ministry to lead bloodlines in the cleansing of iniquities is linked with and important to one's ability to hear the Word of God, see what the plans of the Father are, as opposed to the plans of the enemy and follow with verbal release and co-laboring with the activity of angels," Lydia concluded.

Cleansing of Bloodlines

Next, Ezekiel (who had appeared) began, "This work of your ministry is still foundational. Learn to come quickly to the courts so cases may be ruled upon on their behalf, so legal grounds are removed from enemy plots. The cleansing of bloodline iniquities for this reason is still important. As you continue the work of gaining the courtroom verdicts on your behalf to purge and cleanse iniquities, the enemy is upset to no longer have access to your realm with wrong frequencies. Thus, deluding spirits and lying spirits have a more difficult time twisting, blinding, and duping you. This is why you have felt the importance of emphasizing the cleansing of the bloodlines, as you have been taught."

Cooperating with Messenger Angels

"At present, there are many Messenger Angels that have been released to the saints of God, many more than you can imagine," Ezekiel spoke. "Commission me to work with these Messenger Angels to connect with those in your sphere of influence. The activity right now of Messenger Angels globally is highly active and these Messenger Angels often need assistance from and the protection of other angels as they carry out their duty.

"It is like in wartime, where the lines of communication between generals behind the lines is not the active fighting, but these communication lines must be guarded. Therefore, we offer the following prayer:

Father, we just request in the name of Jesus that these Messenger Angels be given assistance by Ezekiel, his ranks, and commanders, and we asked for backup help for Ezekiel for this? We thank you and commission you to work to protect the Messenger Angels so that they take their communication to the saints so, that no message is lost. We commission you to that in Jesus' name.

"Many of these messengers are being released in the night hours—when you are just drifting to sleep, when you first awake, or they may show up in your dreams," Ezekiel explained. "That seems to be the types of messages that are coming right now that Heaven is talking about. Then the messages, once received, play out during the daylight hours."

Heaven wants to help us understand this, to help us say:

I receive the messages of the Messenger Angels into my realms and into my understanding. I receive the messages. I trust them. And I believe them. They are going to make a difference in the lives of people and in the purpose of God for the planet, and for the purpose of God for the nations. I receive the Messenger Angels who have messages from God that will change the nations. I agree to receive them.

Commission the angels assigned to you to work with Ezekiel, his commanders, and his ranks, as their alignment with the ministry gives us permission to work with your angels. "Sometimes," Ezekiel added, "We stir up their angels or we enlist them as we work together."

Knowing

"The sons of God are learning to see spiritually, and their discernment is improving. These things go hand in hand with knowing who you truly are and how valuable your words are to enact the plans of God.

"One of our activities," Ezekiel pointed out, "is to cause the right word to go to the right ear. We do this often and we often overcome the wrong word to the wrong ear and the wrong word to the right ear."

Protecting Your Ears

Ezekiel continued, "Envision an angel with a sword who sees a wrong word as an object that is traveling in a dimension of space. The angel sees that this word is headed for an ear that should not hear it, so he takes his sword and deflects the word as it goes by, or he may chop it asunder. Therefore, the wrong word does not enter that individual's ear—I am talking about your spirit ear *and* your natural ear. You need angels to help you that your spirit ear and your natural ear do not hear the wrong word—the word that brings doubt, the word that brings fear, the word that brings the activity of iniquity, the word that brings curses, or the word that brings works of darkness."

Angels love their activity of doing this. It is important to agree with one's angels that they are at work doing this well. This is what I mean when the angels of this ministry desire to work with the personal angels assigned to you. They team up together in the spirit realm to better bring down the wrong word. Ezekiel remarked, "Trust me, in this hour, you need our help."

We asked, "Is there a commissioning concerning this?"

"It is always good to commission your personal angels to deflect the wrong words from your ears," he responded.

Remember, you have two sets of ears.

Commission your angels to deflect and bring asunder wrong words that would enter your physical ear and your spiritual ear. This is remarkably like wrong sight.

Protecting Your Eyes

Wrong visuals can enter your spirit eyes and your physical eyes; therefore, you need angels helping you on both.

Protecting Your Heart

After the ears and eyes, there is a matter of the heart.

> *Remember, what your heart longs for*
> *is proof of what your ears have heard,*
> *and your eyes have seen.*

Thus, you are cautioned to focus on the Lord, joyful worship, and gratefulness. Repeating the Words of God enables this, but the work of in the unseen realm is equally important. Commission your personal angels to cut asunder wrong words, declaring that they will not enter your realms, nor will they intersect your pathways, but that you will see and hear guidance from Heaven.

Angels do this equally. They see to the releasing into your sight, and ears, and heart the goodness of the Father, His plans, and His purposes.

> *What angels cannot do*
> *is make agreement for you.*

That is your role. Choose wisely what you will agree with.

"I have not even spoken to you about the element of time for all messages have time elements attached to them. This is true from the kingdom of darkness because it is also true of the Kingdom of Light and has only been stolen and corrupted by the copying of the kingdom of darkness, but do not worry. Angels will see to their task in the unseen and employ their abilities to do what you cannot do. For this reason, they have been assigned to you, even created so that they accomplish things for you," Ezekiel concluded.

Chapter 12
Epilogue

Having read through this book, you now have an understanding of things that were mysteries to you a short time ago. It is our desire for you, but moreover it is the desire of Heaven, that you experience ALL the fulness of God. Paul prayed that for the Ephesian believers and we desire it for you as well. Here is The Mirror Translation of Paul's prayer:

> [16]*I desire for you to realize what the Father has always envisaged for you, so that you may know the magnitude of his [1]intent and be dynamically reinforced in your inner being by the Spirit of God.*

(The word, [1]*doxa, opinion or intent.*)

> [17]*This will ignite your faith to fully grasp the reality of the indwelling Christ. You are rooted and founded in love. Love is your invisible inner source, just like the root system of a tree and the foundation of a building.*

(The dimensions of your inner person exceed any other capacity that could possibly define you.)

18Love is your reservoir of super human 1strength which 2causes you to see everyone equally sanctified in the context of the limitless extent of love's breadth and length and the extremities of its dimensions in depth and height.

(The word, 1*exischuo* means to be entirely competent, to be empowered to 2comprehend. The word 2*katalambano, kata,* strengthened form; with *lambano,* to grasp, thus to entirely grasp, means to come to terms with, to make one's own. Rom 12:13 Purpose with resolve to treat strangers as saints; pursue and embrace them with fondness as friends on equal terms of fellowship. Rom 12:16 Esteem everyone with the same respect; no one is more important than the other. Associate yourself rather with the lowly than with the lofty. Do not distance yourself from others in your own mind. ["Take a real interest in ordinary people."— JB Phillips] In the breadth and length we see the horizontal extent of the love of Christ: the complete inclusion of the human race. 2 Cor 5:14,16. The depth of his love reveals how his love rescued us from the deepest pits of hellish despair and led us as trophies in his triumphant procession on high. Eph 2:5,6, Eph 4:8-10, Col 3:1-4.))

19I desire for you to become intimately acquainted with the love of Christ on the deepest possible level; far beyond the reach of a mere academic, intellectual grasp. Within the scope of this equation God finds the ultimate expression of their image and likeness in you.

(So that you may be filled with all the fullness of God! Awaken to the consciousness of their closeness! Separation is an illusion! Oneness was God's idea all along! Father, Son and Spirit desire to express themselves through your touch, your voice, your presence; they are so happy to dwell in you! There is no place in the universe where God would rather be!)[23] (MIRROR)

To become intimately acquainted with the love of Christ has to occur from the inner realm of our spirit first. As this happens, the reality of what has been done for us in Christ will be unveiled to our soul, which can then begin to cooperate and enjoy partnering with our spirit and body.

It is quite an adventure you have embarked on. May you be able to maximize the revelation we have shared in this book. Pray in the Spirit regularly, not just on special occasions. Tune yourself to the flow of Heaven and hear from Heaven daily. It will change your life.

Colossians 3 in The Mirror Translation defines well the life we are to live and the way we are to live it:

¹See yourselves co-raised with Christ! Now ponder with persuasion the consequence of your co-inclusion in him. Relocate yourselves mentally! Engage your thoughts with throne room realities where you are co-seated with Christ in the executive authority of God's right hand. ²Becoming

---

[23] du Toit, Francois. Mirror Study Bible (pp. 689-690). Kindle Edition.

affectionately acquainted with throne room thoughts will keep you from being distracted again by the earthly [soul-ruled] realm.

("Set your minds upon the things that are above and not upon the things below!" RSV. Whatever you face in your daily lives, acquaint yourselves with the greater reality! The things that are above! Do not engage the energy of the things that are below! Also note Romans 1:18, where the word *katecho* is used - to echo downwards is the opposite to *anoche*, to echo upward- Romans 2:4 and Romans 3:26. Also 2 Corinthians 4:18 "We are not keeping any score of what seems so obvious to the senses on the surface; it is fleeting and irrelevant; it is the unseen eternal realm within us which has our full attention and captivates our gaze!" A renewed mind conquers the space previously occupied by worthless pursuits and habits.

³Your union with his death broke the association with that world; see yourselves located in a fortress where your life is hidden with Christ in God!

("In that day you will know that I am in my Father, and you in me and I in you." [John 14:20] Occupy your mind with this new order of life; you died when Jesus died; whatever defined you before defines you no more. Christ, in whom the fullness of deity dwells, defines you now! The word, "hidden" can also be translated, secret; the secret of your life is your union with Christ in God! [See Col 2:9, 10] "Risen, then, with Christ you must lift your thoughts above where Christ now sits at the right hand of God, you must be heavenly minded; not earthly minded, you have undergone death, and your life is hidden away now with Christ in God. Christ

122

is your life, when he is made manifest you are made manifest in his glory." — Knox Translation.)

⁴The unveiling of Christ, as defining our lives, ¹immediately implies that, what is evident in him, is equally mirrored in you! The exact life on exhibit in Christ is now repeated in us. We are included in the same bliss and joined-oneness with him; just as his life reveals you, your life reveals him.

(This verse was often translated to again delay the revelation of Christ to a future event! The word, ¹otan, often translated as "when" is better translated as "every time." Thus, "Every time Christ is revealed we are being co-revealed in his glory." According to Walter Bauer Lexicon, otan is often used of an action that is repeated. Paul declares our joint-glorification in Christ! We are co-revealed in the same bliss. [See 1 Cor 2:7-8, Rom 3:23-24, Rom 8:30, 2 Pet 1:3.] In him we live and move and have our being; in us he lives and moves and has his being! Acts 17:28.)

⁵Consider the members of your body as dead and buried towards everything related to the porn industry, sensual uncleanness, longing for forbidden things, lust and greed, which are just another form of idol worship.

(Idol worship is worshipping a distorted image of yourself!)

⁶These distorted expressions are in total contradiction to God's design and ¹desire for your life.

(The word [1]*orge*, associated with wrath or punishment is from oregomai, to stretch oneself out, to reach out, to long for, to desire. The sentence, "upon the sons of unbelief" or as the KJV translates it, "sons of disobedience", was added later in some manuscripts.)

[7]*We were all once swept along into a lifestyle of lust and greed. [8]But now, because you realize that you co-died and were co-raised together with Christ, you can flush your thoughts with truth! Permanently put these things behind you: things such as violent outbursts of rage, depression, all manner of wickedness, [1]slander and every form of irregular conversation.*

(The lifelong association with sin is broken; the dominion of the character of God is revealed again in ordinary life. The word [1]blasphemos means any attempt to belittle someone else and to cause someone to receive a bad reputation.)

[9]*That old life was a lie, foreign to our design! Those garments of disguise are now thoroughly stripped off us in our understanding of our union with Christ in his death and resurrection. We are no longer obliged to live under the identity and rule of the robes we wore before, neither are we cheating anyone through false pretensions.*

(The garments an actor would wear define his part in the play but cannot define him.)

[10]*We stand fully identified in the new creation renewed in knowledge according to the pattern of*

the exact image of our Creator. ¹¹The revelation of Christ in us gives identity to the individual beyond anything anyone could ever be as a Greek or a Jew, American or African, foreigner or famous, male or female, king or pawn. From now on everyone is defined by Christ; everyone is represented in Christ.

(In seeing him not just recorded in history but revealed in us, we discover the face of our birth as in a mirror! James 1:18.)

¹²You are the product of God's love; he restored you to his original thought. You belong to him exclusively. It is like changing garments. Now that you have gotten rid of the old, clothe yourselves with inner compassion, kindness, humility, gentleness and patience,

(Just like you were once identified by your apparel, the characteristics of these qualities define you now.)

¹³upholding one another in positive expectation. If anyone finds fault with another, restore that person to favor, remembering how the Lord's forgiveness has transformed our lives. ¹⁴Wear love like a uniform; this is what completes the picture of our oneness. ¹⁵Appoint the peace of Christ as umpire in your hearts. We are all identified in the same person; there is only one body. We are born to be a blessing and exhibit his benevolence. ¹⁶Christ is the language of God's logic. Let his message sink into you with unlimited vocabulary, taking wisdom to its most complete conclusion. This makes your fellowship an environment of instruction in an atmosphere of music. Every lesson is a reminder, echoing in every song you sing, whether it be a ¹psalm or a ²hymn or a ³song in the spirit. Grace fuels your heart with inspired music to the Lord.

(The word ¹*psalmos* is raving about God in praise and worship accompanied by musical instruments. The word ²humnos suggests a celebration in song - a testimony song. An ³*ōdē* en pneumatikos is a new spontaneous spirit chant or song.)

¹⁷Your every conversation and the detail of your daily conduct reflect him; his name and Lordship define your lives and inspire your deep gratitude to God the Father for his grace. ¹⁸His peace is the umpire of your every relationship, especially in the family! Wives, place yourselves in the intimate care of your husbands, acknowledging the lordship of Christ in them. ¹⁹Husbands, love your wives tenderly. Do not exasperate them.

²⁰Children, you display the Christ-life in the way you respond to your parents, keep them glowing with joy, they reflect God's delight in you.

("Parents, don't come down too hard on your children or you'll crush their spirits." — The Message.)

²¹Parents are responsible for the atmosphere at home; avoid vibes that dampen the child's spirit. ²²If you are employed by someone, even having to work like a slave, remember your hearts are ¹intertwined in devotion to God. Don't just look busy when you are being watched, show the same diligence behind your bosses back.

(The word, [1]*haplotes*, from *ha*, particle of union; *hama*, together with + *pleko*, meaning to plait, braid, weave together. See Luke 11:34 "The eye is the lamp of the body; if the eye is single the whole body is full of light!" Entwining our eyes with Papa's eyes is what enlightens our entire being! Which is exactly what the word קוה *Kawa* in Hebrew means in Isaiah 40:31 they that entwine with the Lord's thoughts mount up with wings like eagles! We are wired by design to entwine!)

[23]*Whatever you do, picture Christ in the person you are doing it for; it makes such a difference when you put your heart into it.* [24]*God is no-one's debtor; you are employed under the Lordship of Christ.* [25]*To live contrary to the life of your design is to injure yourself; your job description does not define you, it doesn't matter who you are. Unrighteousness carries its own consequence and it is not a respecter of persons.*[24] *(MIRROR)*

---

[24] du Toit, Francois. Mirror Study Bible (pp. 750-754). Kindle Edition

Description

We must understand that we are first and foremost a spirit being. We have a soul, and both soul and spirit reside in the earthly suits we call our bodies. The primary purpose of your soul is to translate to your body what your spirit is perceiving and help you relate to the 3-D world we live in. We are instructed in Colossians 3 to live from our spirit, as opposed to living from our soulish realm.

Living from our spirit is the way Heaven designed us to live, with our spirit in first place. Having lived most of our lives with our soul out of its proper position, the paradigm of living from our spirit first, spirit forward opens amazing possibilities and enables us to fulfill our destiny, live in peace, and in fellowship with the Father, Son, and Holy Spirit. Join us on the amazing adventure of *Living Spirit Forward!*

About the Author

Dr. Ron Horner is a communicator and author of over twenty books on the subjects of the Courts of Heaven and engaging the realms of Heaven. He teaches through weekly classes, a training program, seminars, and conferences.

Ron is the founder of LifeSpring International Ministries, which serves to advocate for individuals and businesses in the Courts of Heaven. He is also founder of Business Advocate Services (BASGlobal.net), a consulting company with worldwide impact.

Other Books by Dr. Ron M. Horner

Building Your Business from Heaven Down

Building Your Business from Heaven Down 2.0

Cooperating with The Glory

Courts of Heaven Process Charts

Engaging Angels in the Realms of Heaven

Engaging Heaven for Revelation – Volume 1

Engaging the Courts for Ownership & Order

Engaging the Courts for Your City (*Paperback, Leader's Guide & Workbook*)

Engaging the Courts of Healing & the Healing Garden

Engaging the Courts of Heaven

Engaging the Help Desk of the Courts of Heaven

Engaging the Mercy Court of Heaven

Four Keys to Defeating Accusations

Freedom from Mithraism

Let's Get it Right!

Lingering Human Spirits

Overcoming the False Verdicts of Freemasonry

Overcoming Verdicts from the Courts of Hell

Releasing Bonds from the Courts of Heaven

Unlocking Spiritual Seeing